FARMING PERFORMANCE OF FARM WOMEN

About the Author

P.G. Reddy, Associate Professor in Agricultural Extension, is currently working as Deputy Director of Extension, Directorate of Extension, ANGR, Agricultural University, Rajendranagar, Hyderabad. He has put in 22 years of service in ANGR Agricultural University and worked in various capacities in Field Extension, Training, Research, Teaching and Administration.

He also worked as Associate Professor in Extension Education Institute, a regional training institute of Government of India under ANGRAU, where he trained the middle level Extension Functionaries of Line (Development) Departments of Southern India.

Dr. Reddy has guided post-graduate students leading to M.Sc Ph.D. in Extension Education. He has published a dozen research papers in various journals of national repute. He has visited Federal Republic of Germany to participate in 'Appropriate Management and Promotion of Self-Help Organisation during 1993.

His areas of specialisation are Development Communication & Media Strategy; Participatory Rural Appraisal (PRA); Monitoring & Evaluation of Agricultural Programmes and Farming Situation Based Extension.

FARMING PERFORMANCE OF FARM WOMEN

Key to Sustainable Agriculture

P. GIDDA REDDY
Deputy Director of Extension
ANGR Agricultural University,
Rajendranagar, Hyderabad 500030

CONCEPT PUBLISHING COMPANY, NEW DELHI-110059

ISBN 81-8069-022-9

First Published 2003

Published and Printed by
Ashok Kumar Mittal
Concept Publishing Company
A/15-16, Commercial Block, Mohan Garden
New Delhi-110059 (India)
Phones: 25351460, 25351794
Fax: 091–(11)–25357103
E-mail: publishing@conceptpub.com

PREFACE

Women are critical to the well-being of farm households. Rural women have played and continue to play a key role in the conservation of basic life support systems such as land, water, flora and fauna. They have protected the health of the soil through organic recycling and promoted crop security through the maintenance of varietal diversity and genetic resistance. Many households in rural areas are headed by a single parent, usually a mother because men migrate with their limited literacy skills to urban areas for secondary jobs leaving the illiterate women behind with the land and children leading to "feminisation" of agriculture. In reality, women are involved in all aspects of agriculture and allied enterprises, from crop selection to land preparation, seed selection, planting, weeding, harvesting, storage, handling, processing and marketing. Therefore, without the total intellectual and physical participation of women, it will not be possible to popularize farming systems and promote the care of soil and the health of plants and farm animals. Women also tend to look at problems in their totality from sowing of a crop to its ultimate utilization either as food, feed or raw material for industry.

Besides from raising children, rural women are involved in the preparation of food, maintenance of the homestead and assist in crop and animal production by performing various farm activities as already enlisted. These women, despite the fact that they are performing several farm activities/roles, have been over looked by agriculturists and policy makers. A major reason for this is the failure of our developmental planning lies in treating women as "end products" rather than "agents of change". A substantial part of this mystification has occurred because rural women are treated as "farmers' "wives" and not as "farm women".

The present book therefore, demystify the productive role of women in farming systems, a key to sustainable agriculture by analyzing farming performance in terms of their characteristics under the given social framework, role perception, decision-making pattern, etc. The challenge hence lies in integrating brain (technology), brawn (physical work) and bank (credit and other resources) so that farm women can play an active role in improving the productivity, profitability and sustainability of major farming systems.

P. GIDDA REDDY

CONTENTS

LIST OF TABLES

LIST OF FIGURES

1

INTRODUCTION

"A nation would not march forward if the women are left behind."

— *Swamy Vivekananda*

"Rural woman provides human subsidy to the family."

— *Kurukshetra,* November 1987

"We had tongues but could not speak,
We had feet but could not walk,
Now, that we have the land
We have the strength to speak and walk."

— Peasant Women in Bodhgaya, Bihar said when a plot of land allotted in her name in 1982.

"Women grow half of the world's food but own hardly any land,find it difficult to get loans and are overlooked by agricultural advisers and projects. Women are one-third of the world's official labour force but are concentrated in the lowest paid occupations and are more vulnerable to unemployment. Women continue to outnumber men among the world's illiterates by around three to two, 90 per cent of the countries have organisations for promoting the advancement of women but women are under-represented in the decision making bodies."

— *Kurukshetra,* November, 1987

In India, as high as 76 per cent of rural population is engaged in agricultural production and rural women comprise about 50 per cent of agricultural force. There are more than 30 million women working in rural sector, 20 million as agricultural labourers and 10 million employed in animal husbandry, handicrafts and related activities. In the hilly regions of our country female labourers outnumber the male labourers. This is also true in many parts of Tamil Nadu and Andhra Pradesh. In family farm labour, women play an important role in all states in all stages of crop raising, starting from land preparation to harvest and post-harvest processing.

The type and extent of participation by farm women in farm operations vary from state to state, while the participation rate of women in crop production in Haryana, Punjab is only 1.45 and 4.28 per cent respectively. It is higher in Maharashtra and Tamil Nadu, i.e., 29 and 24 per cent respectively and the rate is still higher in North-eastern region and Andhra Pradesh accounting for 70 per cent and 96 per cent respectively (Singh and Battacharya, 1990).

On the threshold of the twenty-first century, we find that the condition of our women folk, particularly those of rural community is still very deplorable. In view of the tremendous contribution that women are making and can yet make, it is not a matter of little concern, rather time has come when it has been realised that, for speedy and overall development of agriculture, their involvement needs to be properly assessed and known. In the production oriented programmes for rural development, there has been very little or practically no effort to evaluate the role played by the rural women.

The human development report for 1995, published by UNDP, the findings of a 31-country study, women work longer hours than men—on an average women put in 13 per cent more time than men in developing countries and 6 per cent more than men in developed countries. Another finding is that of the total burden of work—women carry 53 per cent and men 47 per cent in developing countries and the figures are 51 per cent and 49 per cent respectively for developed countries (Kurukshetra, 1995).

Today, 44 per cent of world's food is produced by women

which indicates how important their role is in farming. Rural women in general and farm women in particular are engaged in different activities. Despite their substantial contributions women continue to be marginalised, undervalued and unrecognised. There is a tendency among most administrators and policy makers to see "men as farmers" and "women as farmer's wives" and highlight their 'supportive role' rather than their 'productive role' (Samantha, 1994).

Further, recent studies reveal that 50-90 per cent of agricultural operations are carried out by women only. It can, therefore, be forcefully established that their contribution to agriculture and allied activities in rural India is immense.

The farming system approach has been used recently in an effort to increase agricultural land productivity and farmer welfare. The animal husbandry and crop production enterprises in a farming system are interlinked, complimentary and interdependent and provide gainful employment to the farm women throughout the year. The income from livestock is relatively assured than from crop enterprises which largely depend on the vagaries of nature.

The basic socio-economic units in rural development are not farmers alone but rural households including all activities, income resources and problems of their members. Recognition of this is a necessary element in the formulation and implementation of appropriate and realistic farming system programmes. At the present time attempts to develop the role of women, which reflect on improved social status, imply on orientation towards greater integration of women into development and basically emphasise on three main aspects, i.e., integration in production, reproduction process and participation in decision-making process (Pudjiwati, 1987).

Hence, the challenge lies in integrating brain (technology), brawn (physical work) and bank (credit) in a mutually supportive manner so that both men and women can play an active role in improving the productivity, profitability, stability and sustainability of major farming systems.

Need and importance of the study

Several farming systems are in vogue in Andhra Pradesh and rice based farming system [by integrating enterprises, viz., agriculture (rice), horticulture (vegetables) and animal husbandry (dairy and poultry) is one of the popular farming systems existing in Ranga Reddy district of Andhra Pradesh. It is apparent that farm women are involved in several farm related activities in the rice based farming system.

The main issue was to what extent these farm women were involved in role performance and in decision-making of farm related activities to improve their farming performance in rice based farming system. In recent years, several studies have been conducted on farm women who carry out agricultural operations as an agricultural labour or as a member of family workforce. But hardly any attention was paid to the farm women who are "principal farmers" in spite of their participation in agriculture in Andhra Pradesh is 70-96 per cent (Singh, K.N., 1990). Hence, farm women were considered as respondents for the present study.

Duly keeping in mind the importance of women in agriculture and allied activities, this study was undertaken to analyse the roles and farming performance of farm women in rice based farming system with special reference to Ranga Reddy district of Andhra Pradesh. This study was constituted to answer some of the questions like, what are the personal, socio-psychological and extension related characteristics of farm women? What was their role performance and perception about roles in rice based farming system? The extent of their farming performance and the relationship of independent variables with farming performance of farm women. The following specific objectives were formulated to answer the issues raised above.

General objective

To study the roles and farming performance of farm women in a rice based farming system.

Specific objectives of the study

1. To find out the personal, socio-psychological and extension related characteristics of different groups of farm women in rice based farming system;
2. To ascertain the roles performed by different groups of farm women;
3. To study the role perception of farm women and their husbands;
4. To identify the areas and decision making pattern of different groups of farm women;
5. To measure the farming performance of different groups of farm women in rice based farming system; and
6. To ascertain the relationship between the farming performance and selected characteristics of farm women, if any, in rice based farming system.

2

LITERATURE

The present research is concerned with the roles and farming performance of farm women in rice based farming system. There is paucity of literature on the farming performance of farm women. However, a brief available literature has been reviewed in accordance with the objectives set forth for the study and is presented under the following sub-heads:

Scope of rice based farming system.
Personal, socio-psychological and extension related characteristics of farm women.
Roles performed by farm women in rice based farming system.
Role perception of farm women and their husbands.
Areas and decision making pattern of farm women in a rice based farming system.
Farming performance of farm women.
Relationship of characteristics of farm women with farming performance.
Conceptual framework and derivation of hypothesis.

Scope of rice based farming system

Mandal *et al.* (1989) stated that farming system is wholistic as the whole farm is viewed as a system encompassing interacting sub-systems. No potential enterprise is considered in isolation. It looks at the farm family household as a system of natural and human components.

Raman and Balaguru (1990) reported that farming system, as a concept, takes into account the components of soil, water, crops, livestock, labour and other resources with the farm family at the centre managing agricultural and related activities.

Swaminathan (1990) opined that farming system aims to optimise the income and employment potential of the small farm through concurrent attention to crop and animal husbandry and post-harvest technologies, needs to be more widely fostered.

Personal, socio-psychological and extension related characteristics of farm women

Age : Suchitra (1987) concluded that majority (71.66%) of farm women belonged to middle age group followed by young (14.16%) and old age (14.76%).

Puneetha (1989) observed that majority (71.25%) of farm women fell in the middle age category followed by young (17.5%) and old age (11.25%) categories.

Education : Padma (1987) concluded that majority (70%) of respondents belonged to the illiterate category followed by 28.34 per cent and 1.66 per cent had primary and high school education.

Reddy (1990) observed that 65 per cent of the farm women were illiterate followed by 15 per cent can read, 10 per cent can read and write, 6 per cent had primary education and only 4 per cent had middle school education.

Farm size : Sabitakumari (1995) observed that majority (65.83%) of the women respondents owned small farms while 13.33 per cent respondents had large farms, 10.84 per cent had medium size farms.

Farming experience : Sreedevi (1996) reported that majority (54.17%) of farm women had high farming experience followed by medium (25%) and low (20.83%) experience in farming.

Material possession : Umadevi (1992) reported that majority of the trained and untrained farm women fell in the middle category (35%) of material possession followed by low (4.17%) and high (30.83%).

Annual income : Rajini (1989) reported that majority of farm women (41.67%) belonged to low income group, while 26.64 per cent and 31.70 per cent belonged to medium and high income categories.

Reddy (1996) observed in his study that majority of the dairy farmers belonged to medium level income category.

Social participation : Suchitra (1987) concluded that majority of the women respondents (70%) had no social participation and 30 per cent participated in social activities.

Sabitakumari (1995) reported that majority (97.5%) of rural women had no membership in any social organisation whereas 1.67 per cent had present membership in one organisation and 0.84 per cent had membership in the past.

Innovativeness : Surgeon (1989) reported that majority (64.16%) of farmers had medium innovativeness while 20.84 per cent belonged to low innovativeness category and the rest of 15 per cent had high innovativeness.

Shailaja (1990) observed that large farm women were significantly superior to other three categories of farm women. No significant difference was observed between small and marginal farm women, however, they were superior to women agricultural labour.

Self-confidence : Surgeon (1989) reported that majority of (57.5%) farmers belonged to medium self-confidence category followed by 21.67 per cent low and 20.83 per cent high self-confidence categories.

Level of aspiration : Shailaja (1990) reported that marginal farm women had a high level of aspiration and were superior to large and small farm women. There was no significant difference between large and small farm women with respect to level of aspiration.

Umadevi (1992) observed that 35.83 per cent of farm women belonged to medium category followed by high (33.33%) and low (30.83%).

Scientific orientation : Shailaja (1990) observed that there is no significant difference between large and small farm women in respect of scientific orientation. Small farm women differ significantly with agricultural labour but not with marginal farm women.

Achievement motivation : Sabitakumari (1995) found that majority (71.67%) of the rural women had medium achievement motivation. Whereas, 19.17 per cent had high and 9.16 per cent low achievement motivation.

Economic orientation : Uma Devi (1992) observed that majority of farm women fell in the 'medium' category (46.67%), followed by high (31.67%) and low (21.67%) categories of economic orientation.

Risk preference : Umadevi (1992) observed that majority of farm women fell under 'medium' category (59.17%) followed by high (23.33%) and low (17.5%) categories of risk preference

Rationality in decision making: Rao (1985) found that majority of farmers (44%) had medium/moderate decision making rationality.

Surgeon (1989) observed that majority of the farmers (58.83%) belonged to medium rational decision making ability followed by 27.5 per cent high and 14.17 per cent low rational decision making ability categories.

Extension contact : Umadevi (1992) observed that almost equal per cent of farm women belonged to medium and low extension contact categories (35.83% and 35% respectively) followed by high category (29.17%).

Extension participation : Umadevi (1992) in her study stated that 35.83 per cent of farm women had medium extension participation, while 35 per cent were in low extension participation category.

Information seeking : Goud (1990) found that majority (44.4%) of respondents had high level of information seeking behaviour followed by medium (36.7%) and low (18.9%).

Training : Sreedevi (1996) observed that none of the farm women had received training.

Roles performed by women in rice based farming system

Bhuyan *et al.* (1988) reported that women have performed their roles in sowing, transplanting and weeding operations and also they worked with men in operations like harvesting, threshing and storage.

Ghosh *et al.* (1988) reported that women role performance in farm operations in West Bengal ranged from 28 to 44 per cent in case of threshing and winnowing, 24 to 58 per cent in case of seed storage.

Singh *et al.* (1988) reported that majority of farm operations were performed by the women in hill areas while their husbands migrate to plains in search of work.

Role perception of farm women and their husbands

Lakshmi Devi (1983) stated that there was significant differences in perception of rural women and their husbands in relation to farm and home activities.

Areas and decision making pattern of farm women in rice based farming system

Shailaja (1990) reported that majority of farm women in different categories (50% of large farm women; 56% of small farm women and 65% of marginal farm women) participated in decision making areas such as, choice of crops, seed selection, storage of produces, care and management of animals and number of animals to be maintained.

Sabitakumari (1995) stated that 64.6 per cent of the women respondents belonged to medium decision making category followed by low (28.33%) and high (7.5%) decision making category.

Farming performance of farm women

Shailaja (1990) observed that there was no significant difference between large and small farm women in mixed farming productivity but they differ significantly with other two categories, i.e., marginal and agricultural labour.

Sreedevi (1996) reported that majority (74.17%) of the farm women belonged to medium cropping intensity category followed by low (15%) and high (10.83%) cropping intensity.

She also observed that majority (90.83%) of the farm women fell under medium crop yield index category, while 6.67 per cent had low and 2.5 per cent high crop yield index category.

Sreedevi (1996) stated that 65.83 per cent of farm women had medium level of adoption followed by low (19.17%) and high (15%) level of adoption categories.

She also reported in her study, that majority (92.5%) of farm women belonged to medium commercialization category, while 7.5 per cent had low commercialisation index.

Further, she also stated that majority (90.83%) of the farm women belonged to low expansion/diversification category followed by medium (6.67%) and high (2.5%) categories.

Relationship of characteristics of farm women with farming performance

Sreedevi (1996) reported that 'age', 'achievement motivation' and 'socio-politico participation' had no significant association but observed 'training', 'information seeking behaviour', 'extension contact' and 'education' had positive significant relationship with the farming performance of farm women.

Shailaja (1990) found that 'education', 'farm size', 'income', 'innovation proneness', 'scientific orientation', 'achievement motivation', 'economic motivation', 'extension participation', 'decision making', and 'role performance', has shown positive and significant relationship with mixed farming productivity of farm women. She also reported that 'level of aspiration' has no relationship with the mixed farming productivity of farm women.

Umadevi (1992) reported no significant relationship existed between 'material possession' and adoption of recommended practices of farm women.

Goud (1990) observed a positive and significant correlation between 'farm experience' and farming performance of farmers.

Rao (1985) in his study reported that the scores of 'self-confidence' and farming performance of farmers was found to be significant at 0.01 level of probability.

Reddy (1990) found that 'risk preference' of dairy farmers has not significantly related with the adoption of dairy production technologies, but was in a positive direction.

INFERENCES FROM REVIEW

1. Farm women performed majority of the roles in rice based farming system.
2. Farm women actively participated in most of the areas of decision making while performing farming activities.
3. Farming performance in rice based farming system is a multidimensional concept with several components, viz., cropping intensity, crop yield index, milk yield index, adoption

level, commercialisation index and expansion/diversification index.

4. Farm women perceived the identified roles in the rice based farming system as very important.
5. Certain charaoteristics of farm women found to have relationship with the farming performance.

Conceptual Framework and Derivation of Hypothesis

Conceptual model : In the light of the inferences derived from the literature, conceptual framework was developed for the study which diagramatically represents the important dimensions and postulated relationships among the variables.

The dependent variable of the study farming performance was supposed to be a function of a number of independent variables. Twenty-one independent variables representing personal, socio-psychological and extension related characteristics of farm women were chosen based on the review and in consultation with the experts to examine the extent of relationship with the farming performance in rice based farming system. The proposed relationships are represented in a conceptual model (Fig.1) which helped to derive hypotheses for empirical testing.

Derivation of hypotheses : The following thcorctical, general and sub-general hypotheses were derived based on the theoretical orientation and relationships.

Theoretical hypothesis : The farming performance of farm women vary with and can, in part, be predicted from their personal, socio-psychological and extension related characteristics.

General hypothesis : There will be an association between farming performance of farm women and their personal, socio-psychological and extension related characteristics.

Sub-general hypothesis-1 : There will be a relationship between

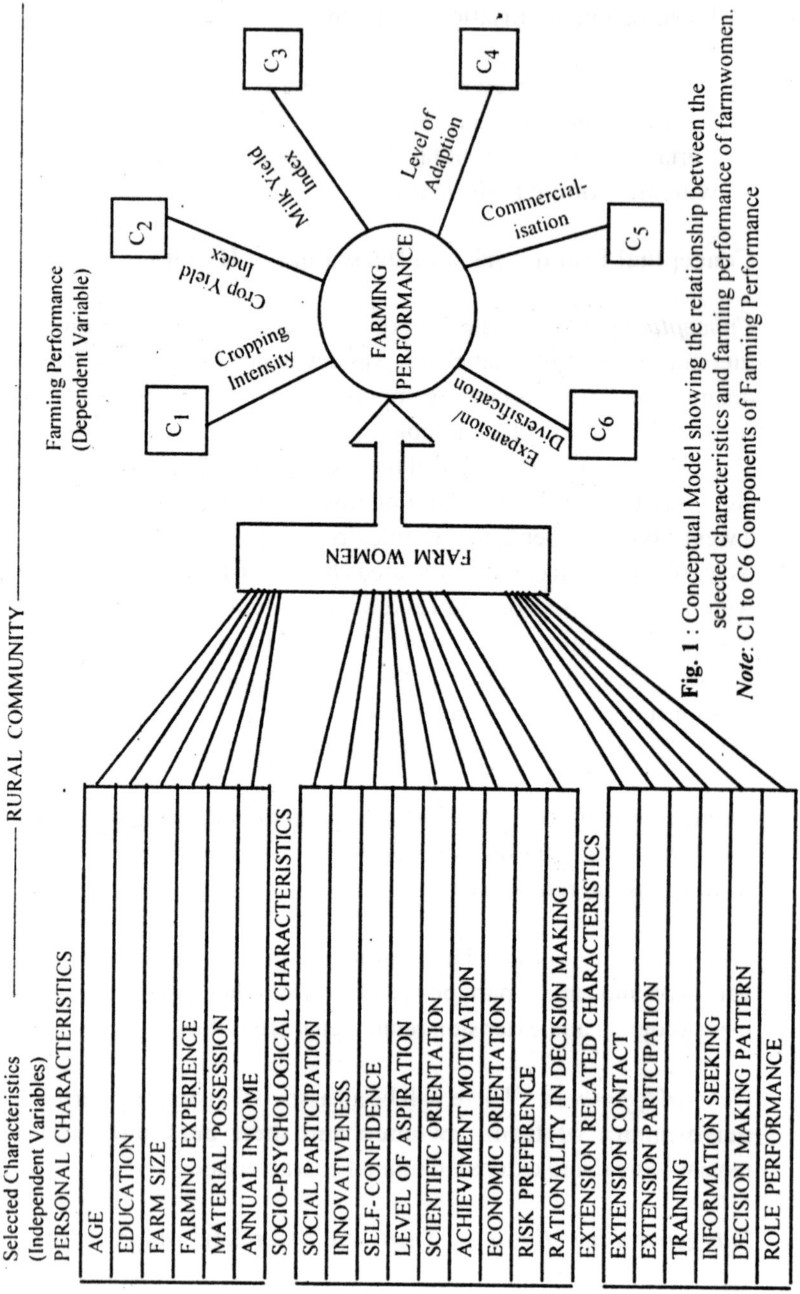

Fig. 1 : Conceptual Model showing the relationship between the selected characteristics and farming performance of farmwomen.

Note: C1 to C6 Components of Farming Performance

personal characteristics and farming performance of farm women.

Sub-general hypothesis-2 : There will be a relationship between socio-psychological characteristics and farming performance of farm women.

Sub-general hypothesis-3 : There will be a relationship between extension related characteristics and farming performance of farm women.

Operationalisation of Concepts Used

Farm woman : It is operationalised as the woman who possesses family agricultural land and involved in the crop production and animal husbandry activities on her family farm.

Rice based farming system: is operationalised as those women who practice a farming system keeping rice as a base crop and integrating with other land based enterprises, namely, horticulture (vegetables), and animal husbandry (dairy/poultry) by utilising the available farm resources to earn an increased annual income to sustain their family living in a better way.

Role perception: is operationalised as the reaction of farm women and their husbands towards the expected roles of farm women as most important, important and least important in a rice based farming system.

Note : Statement of hypothesis under sub-general hypothesis involving each independent variable in relation to dependent variable has not been done for the sake of brevity and also to avoid redundancy in statements.

3

RESEARCH METHODOLOGY

This chapter deals with the research design, locale of the study, sample and sampling procedures, variables and their measurement, collection of data, statistical methods and analytical procedures followed to interpret the results of the investigation.

Research design

Ex post facto research design was used since the variables chosen for the investigation had already resulted in cause and effect relationship.

Locale of the study

Andhra Pradesh State was selected purposively because :

(a) Andhra Pradesh is one of the states where land based enterprises (viz., agriculture, horticulture, fisheries sericulture and animal husbandry) are predominant occupation of the people.
(b) Andhra Pradesh State's rural female population is practically involved in almost all the farm and allied operations.
(c) The researcher belonged to the state of Andhra Pradesh.

Sample and sampling procedure

Selection of the district : Ranga Reddy district was selected purposively on the following criteria:

(a) The district was and is exposed to modernisation of land based activities very intensively as a host of agricultural research and development organisations are located.
(b) ANTWA (Andhra Pradesh Training of Women in Agriculture), a special project to train women farmers was started in this district with a view to improve their farming performance in agriculture and allied activities.
(c) The district has well and tank irrigation facilities where rice is the predominant cereal crop. The district stands second in vegetable production in the state. Since the district is very close to Hyderabad city, dairy and poultry are the major subsidiary occupations/enterprises of the farmers, thus indicating a comprehensive farming systems approach.
(d) The investigator is working at Extension Education Institute located in the district which was more convenient for the investigator to conduct in-depth analysis of socio-psychological factors influencing the farming performance of farm women, and also familiar with the local colloquial language.

Selection of mandals : The list of mandals in Ranga Reddy district was obtained from the "Bureau of Economics and Statistics", Government of Andhra Pradesh. Out of 37 mandals, six mandals viz., Ibrahimpatnam, Medchel, Shankarapally, Shahbad, Marpally and Darur were selected by simple random technique.

Selection of villages : There are 183 villages in six mandals. Two villages from each mandal, viz., Yeliminedu, Polkampally, Athevelle, Gundlapochampalli, Chendippa, Dhobipet, Kakuloor, Damerapally, Marpally, Ravalapally, Sultanpur and Chityal, making a total of 12 villages were selected by using simple random sampling method.

The map of Ranga Reddy district with Mandals and villages selected for the study is shown in Fig. 2.

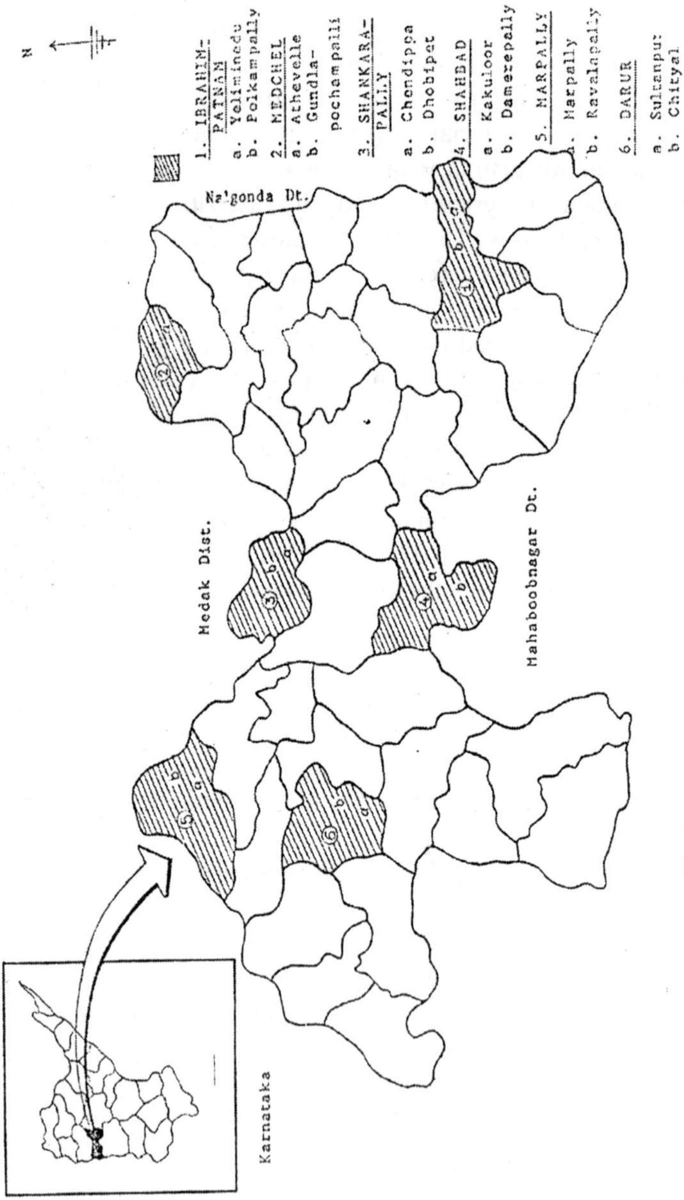

Fig. 2 : Ranga Reddy District Map showing Mandals and Villages.

Selection of farm women : The list of farm families and farm women were obtained from the Village Assistant and VEO (Village Extension Officer) records. Rice based farming system with the three enteprises, viz., agriculture (rice), horticulture (vegetables) and animal husbandry (dairy/poultry) is very predominant in the district in general and in the selected farm families in particular. The farm women thus listed were stratified into three categories, viz., large, medium and small farm women depending on the possession of land. A sample size of 180 was selected from the three farm women groups drawn from 12 villages by employing proportionate stratified random sampling method. Details of farm women and sampling procedure are furnished in Table 1.

Variables and their measurement

Table 2 shows the variables selected and their empirical measurement.

Dependent variable

Farming performance : The criterion variable "farming performance" was conceptualised as the farming productivity behaviour of farm women in a farming system.

The investigator in the present study has used the farming performance index developed by Rao (1985) with modifications. The farming performance consisted of five factors/components, viz., crop yield index, cropping intensity, level of adoption, commercialisation index and expansion/diversification index.

Since the present study was on a farming systems approach, the investigator included the sixth component 'Milk yield index', thus, in all, six components were selected which formed the farming performance of farm women on the suggestion of experts.

Table 1 : Distribution of population and sample selected for the study

Mandal	Village	Population				Sample selected			
		Small	Medium	Large	Total	Small	Medium	Large	Total
Ibrahampatnam	1. Yeliminedu	205	204	100	509	7	7	3	17
	2. Polkampally	214	150	64	428	7	5	2	14
Medchel	1. Athevelle	128	90	38	256	4	3	1	8
	2. Gundlapochampally	329	230	99	658	11	9	3	23
Shankarapally	1. Chendippa	87	61	27	175	3	2	1	6
	2. Dhobipet	535	375	160	1070	16	12	5	33
Shahbad	1. Kakuloor	343	240	103	686	12	8	3	23
	2. Damerepally	129	90	38	257	5	3	1	9
Marpally	1. Marpally	374	262	12	748	13	9	3	
	2. Ravalapally	108	75	32	215	4	2	1	7
Darur	1. Sultanpur	118	82	35	235	4	3	1	8
	2. Chityal	100	70	30	200	4	2	1	7
Total		2670	1929	838	5437	90	65	25	180

Table 2 : Variables and their measurement

S.No.	Variable		Empirical measurement
A.	**Dependent variable**		
1.	Farming performance of Farm women	—	Index developed by V.G.K. Rao (1985) with modification.
B.	**Independent variables**		
(a)	*Personal characteristics :*		
1.	Age	—	Completed years of respondents.
2.	Education	—	Socio-economic status scale of Venkataramaiah (1983), revised in (1990).
3.	Farm size	—	-do-
4.	Farming experience	—	No. of years the farm women had been in farming.
5.	Material possession	—	Socio-economic status scale of Venkataramaiah (1990).
6.	Annual income	—	Structured schedule developed for the study.
(b)	*Socio-psychological characteristics :*		
7.	Social participation	—	Socio-economic status scale of Venkataramaiah (1990).
8.	Innovativeness	—	Scale developed by Feaston (1968) modified by Bhati and Bhatnagar (1972) and Rao (1985b).
9.	Self-confidence	—	Scale developed by Basavanna (1971) and Prasad (1983) subsequently modified by Rao (1985) was adopted.
10.	Level of aspiration	—	Procedure developed by Seema (1986).
11.	Scientific orientation	—	Scale developed by Supe (1969) modified by Sailaja (1990) was used.
12.	Achievement motivation	—	Scale of Prasad (1983) adopted by Sailaja (1990) was used.
13.	Economic orientation	—	Scale of Supe (1969) modified by Sailaja (1990) was used.

(Contd.)

Table 2 : *(Contd.)*

S.No.	Variable		Empirical measurement
14.	Risk preference	—	Scale of Supe (1969).
15.	Rationality in decision making	—	Scale of Supe (1969) subsequently modified by Rao (1985).
(c)	*Extension related characteristics:*		
16.	Extension contact	—	Procedure developed by Byra Reddy (1971) with modifications.
17.	Extension participation	—	-do-
18.	Training undergone	—	Schedule developed for the study.
19.	Information seeking	—	Procedure developed by Rao (1985).
20.	Decision making pattern	—	Schedule developed for the study.
21.	Role performance and role perception of farm women and their husbands	—	Schedule developed for the study.

Measurement of Farming Performance Factors

Procedure adopted for the measuring each component of farming performance is given below :

Cropping intensity (CI) : It was defined operationally as the proportion of total annual cropped area in acres to the total size of holding in acres expressed in percentage. It was calculated by the formula :

$$CI = \frac{\text{Total annual cropped area in acres}}{\text{Size of holding in acres}} \times 100$$

Crop yield index (CYI) : The index represents the yield of all crops on the farm compared with the average crop yields of the region.

The crop yield index of the farm was calculated by dividing the yield per acre of each crop by the average yield of the crop in the region and multiplied by 100 to get percentage index. By using the area devoted to each crop on the farm as a weight to multiply this percentage index, the products are obtained. Finally, adding the products and dividing the sum of the products by the total cropped area (in acres) on the farm, the crop yield index was obtained. An example of calculation of crop yield index is given as follows :

Example of crop yield index calculation (CYI)

Name of the farm woman: B. Lakshmi Devi, W/o B. Gopal Reddy
Village : Polkampalli

S.No.	Crop	Area (Ac)	Yield in q/ac.		Crop Yield as per cent (4/5 × 100)	Percentage × No. of acres (Cols. 6 × 3)
			In your farm	Mandal average		
1	2	3	4	5	6	7
1.	Paddy	6.0	18.0	19.0	$\frac{18}{19} \times 100 = 94.7$	94.7 × 6 =568.2
2.	Jowar	5.0	2.5	2.3	$\frac{2.5}{2.3} \times 100 = 108.6$	108.6 × 5 = 543
3.	Castor	3.0	3.0	1.7	$\frac{3.0}{1.7} \times 100 = 176.0$	176.0 × 3 = 528
4.	Sunflower	4.0	3.0	2.0	$\frac{3.0}{2.5} \times 100 = 120.0$	120.0 × 4 = 480
5.	Tomato	—1.5	36.0	31.5	$\frac{36}{31.5} \times 100 = 114.0$	114 × 1.5 = 171
	Total	9.5				2290.2

$$\text{CYI} = \frac{\text{Total of Column 7}}{\text{Total of Column 3}} = 2290.2/19.5$$

$$\text{CYI} = 119.28\%$$

Milk yield index (MYI) : The procedure adopted is similar to crop yield index and an example of calculation is shown as:

Name of the farm woman: B. Lakshmi Devi, W/o B. Gopal Reddy
Village : Polkampalli.

S.No.	Type of animals	No. of animals	Yield in Lit/animal/day.		Milk yield in % (4/5 × 100)	Percentage No. of animals (Cols. 6 × 3)
			Milk yield of your animal	Village average		
1	2	3	4	5	6	7
1.	Buffalo	2	2.0	2.5	$\frac{2}{2.5} \times 100 = 80$	80 × 2 = 160
2.	Cow	1	1.5	2.0	$\frac{1.5}{2.0} \times 100 = 75$	75 × 1 = 75
Total		3				235

$$\text{MYI} = \frac{\text{Total of column 7}}{\text{Total of column 3}} = \frac{235}{3} = 78.33\%$$

Level of adoption : The individual farmers' level of adoption was calculated by taking into consideration the recommended practices followed for the principal crops grown on her farm and dairy. Adoption quotient is calculated by the following formula:

$$\text{Level of adoption} = \frac{\text{Number of practices adopted}}{\text{No. of crops grown} \times \text{No. of practices}} \times 100$$

Commercialisation index : The index of commercialisation was arrived at by calculating the percentage of produce sold as suggested by Roy *et al.* (1968). The following formula was used for calculating the degree of commercialisation:

$$\text{Commercialisation index} = \frac{\text{Value of farm produce sold}}{\text{Gross value of all production on the farm}} \times 100$$

Expansion/diversification was operationally conceived in this study as the degree of expansion/diversification of farm and establishment of farm and other enterprises such as dairy, poultry, etc., from the time of one's involvement.

For arriving at a score of expansion, the investment made by the respondent since her involvement in the farming on the following items were considered.

Expansion	Acres	Investment made (Rs.)
Farm Enterprise		
1. *Agriculture*		
(a) Dryland	—	—
(b) Irrigated dry	—	—
(c) Wet land	—	—
2. *Animal husbandry*		
(a) Dairy animal	—	—
(b) Poultry	—	—
3. *Off farm enterprise*		
(a) Vegetable business	—	
(b) Small grocery shop	—	—
(c) Small flour mill	—	—

The cost incurred on items by the respondent was found out

and the total investment was arrived. Among 180 respondents, the maximum investment made by the respondent was taken as criterion and each respondent's investment was expressed in percentage to the investment. Thus, relevancy weightage was obtained on the expansion/diversification index for each respondent.

$$\text{Expansion/diversification Index (EDI)} = \frac{\text{Investment made by the respondent}}{\text{Maximum investment in the sample}} \times 100$$

The total farming performance index for each respondent was obtained by adding up the indices obtained on each component. The indices obtained for each component was transformed into another scale, viz., 'Z' scores which followed the linear relationship to enable mathematical operations. The Z scores obtained under each component were summated to obtain the farming performance score of all respondents. Thus, the data approximately followed the normal distribution and hence, the data fits for application of parametric statistical tests.

Based on the farming performance scores, the farm women were categorised using mean and standard deviation.

Category

Low	—	Below (Mean – 1 SD)
Medium	—	Between (Mean ± 1 SD)
High	—	Above (Mean + 1 SD)

Independent variables

The characteristics of farm women were considered as independent variables in the study. Based on extensive review of past studies, various characteristics of farm women were collected and grouped under different sub-heads. The opinion of experts was sought on the relevance or otherwise of these characteristics for the study of farm women in relation to their farming performance. Based on their relevance as judged by the experts, twenty-one characteristics were selected. The rank order of characteristics along with their average scores as judged by the experts is given in Appendix-I. These independent variables were quantified by following the procedures as indicated in Table 2.

Data Collection

In the present study data was collected in two stages. The first stage consisted of collecting data regarding the variables to be selected for the study from extension experts of NIRD, MANAGE, NAARM and EEI. For the roles which farm women could perform and the delineation of the areas of decision making in rice based farming system, the items to be included were collected and relevancy testing was done by the Subject Matter Specialists of A.P.A.U. and Agricultural and Veterinary officers of A.P. State.

For the second stage of data collection, an interview schedule was prepared to achieve the objectives set for the study and the factual data was collected from the farm women by the researcher which was subjected to statistical analysis.

4

RESULTS AND DISCUSSION

The objective of this investigation was to critically analyse the components of farming performance and overall farming performance of different categories of farm women in rice based farming system in Ranga Reddy district of Andhra Pradesh. The study also focused on the roles performed by farm women and their decision making pattern. It also aimed at the perception of farm women and their husbands on the expected roles of farm women. The investigation further focused on the probable personal, socio-psychological and extension related characteristics that influence the farming performance of farm women in rice based farming system.

Keeping the objectives of the study in mind, the empirical evidences obtained in terms of factual data has been analysed by subjecting them to appropriate statistical tests. The findings and discussions are presented objectivewise in this chapter.

Personal, socio-psychological and extension related characteristics of farm women.
Roles performed by different groups of farm women in rice based farming system.
Role perception of different groups of farm women and their husbands in selected enterprises in a rice based farming system.
Areas and decision making pattern of different groups of farm women in a rice based farming system.
Farming performance of different groups of farm women.
Relationship between personal, socio-psychological and

extension related characteristics with the farming performance of farm women.

SECTION – A

PERSONAL, SOCIO-PSYCHOLOGICAL AND EXTENSION RELATED CHARACTERISTICS OF FARM WOMEN

Personal variables

Age : Out of the total respondents (pooled sample) selected for the study majority (70%) of farm women belonged to middle age group (36-55 years), nearly 19.4 per cent to young age (upto 35 years) and around 10.6 per cent old age group (above 55 years). Age should be considered while formulating development programmes related to agriculture and allied enterprises which would enhance the farming performance as women at middle age are relatively free from domestic responsibilities (like taking care of children etc.) when compared to young women and more enthusiastic when compared with old women. The findings was in line with the findings of Suchitra (1987) and Puneetha (1989).

Education : Majority (50.6%) of farm women were illiterate followed by can read only (33.3%) and a very small per cent of farm women (14.4%) can read and write too. The women particularly rural women, have been neglected since ages because of male domination and is being continued even today. Moreover, the rural women start working on the farm at an early age leaving no time for their education. Hence, more efforts are needed to change the outlook of both women and men towards the importance of education which certainly empower farm women to involve more actively and produce better farming performance. The result is in line with that of Padma (1987) and Sabitakumari (1995).

Farm size : 50 per cent of the selected farm women belonged to small farm women category followed by medium (36.1%) and large (13.9%) farm women. In rural areas joint families break into nucleus families resulting in the division of land and hence more number of small farm families. It gives an insight to the development agencies of government and non-government to formulate integrated land based activities to support them economically based on their farm size and the available resources. The result is similar to that of Sabitakumari (1995).

Farming experience : The pooled sample of farm women revealed that 48.3 per cent had 18-28 years of farming experience falling in medium category followed by low (45.6%) of 6-17 years and high category (6.1%) of above 28 years experience. The 18-28 years of farming experience could be considered as sufficient exposure to farming by any standard and possibility of understanding and analysing the farm activities to improve their performance. The finding draws support from Sridevi (1996).

Material possession : More than half of farm women (56.1%) had low material possession followed by medium material possession category (31.7%) in this investigation. The finding was in the expected direction as the sample consists of 50 per cent of small farm women. The small farm women with less land holding spend their maximum manual labour involving more drudgery in cultivating their farms without much dependence on improved implements leading to low material possession. The result was in conformity with that of Umadevi (1992).

Annual income : A great majority (70.6%) of farm women belonged to medium income category followed by low (17.8%) and high (11.6%) income categories. Since the respondents selected had more than one enterprise which could have generated a reasonable income to live with indicating scope for women to perform under the integrated farming situations.

Socio-psychological variables

Social participation : Among the selected respondents, nearly 79.4 per cent of farm women did not have any social participation followed by 20.6 per cent participated in one or more organisations. The farm women were ignorant and never knew any organisation outside their farm and home. There is a need to make them aware and participate in the existing social institutions to broaden their outlook. The finding was similar to Suchitra (1987) and Sabitakumari (1995).

Innovativeness : In the given sample of respondents, around 60.6 per cent belonged to medium category with regard to innovativeness while 22.8 per cent were in low and 16.6 per cent in high category of innovativeness. Generally, innovativeness involves an element of risk and moreover, innovations would be adopted only after their success is established and hence most of them fell under medium category in adopting innovations. The result was in agreement with Surgeon (1989).

Self-confidence : The pooled sample of farm women indicated that 55.6 per cent of them found to be in medium category in respect of self-confidence, while 33.3 per cent in low and 11.1 per cent in high category of self-confidence. Women, particularly the rural women, had been suppressed or subjugated for a long time leaving no chance to show their potential and hence fell under medium category of self-confidence and the finding drew support from Surgeon (1989).

Level of aspiration : Nearly half (45.6%) of farm women had low level of aspiration followed by medium level of aspiration category (38.3%). This might be due to lack of awareness and knowledge of avenues for their improvement to plan for future and live better. The result was in agreement with that of Umadevi (1992).

Scientific orientation : The composite picture of all the farm women revealed that nearly half of them (46.7%) belonged to medium category in respect of scientific orientation towards farm related activities. Farm women acquire knowledge related to agriculture and allied technologies, evaluate them objectively and adopt them to get increased returns from their land obviously indicating that farm women has the potential to evaluate any activity objectively (i.e., analytical capacity) in a more systematic or scientific way. The result was in consonant with that of Shailaja (1990).

Achievement motivation : Nearly 67.8 per cent of farm

women reported to be falling in the medium category in respect of achievement motivation in farm related activities. Achievement motivation mentally mobilises human beings to act upon their active needs and compel them to move forward and achieve their goals. The inner drive of farm women might have gained an urge to achieve better farming performance to improve their standards of living and thus confirming the finding of Sabitakumari (1995).

Economic orientation : The aggregate data of all farm women together revealed that 62.8 per cent of them had medium economic orientation in rice based farming system. This might be due to different combination of enterprises of economic importance available under rice based farming system as the farm women rightly realised that income from agriculture alone was not sufficient to lead reasonably good life and hence developed economic orientation in evaluating farming enterprises. Similar finding was reported by Umadevi (1992).

Risk preference : Out of the total respondents, 51.7 per cent of farm women reported to have fell in the medium category in respect of risk preference followed by low (31.7%) and high (16.6%) categories of risk preference. Risk preference is the cognitive aspect of change which reflect the preparedness of an individual to accept innovations with an element of risk in farm activities. The farm women in this investigation who wanted to reap windfall profits from innovations, an element of risk taking was inevitable as the technologies or innovations fast becoming obsolete and hence preferred to take little risk. The finding was in agreement with that of Umadevi (1992).

Rationality in decision making : Majority (45.6%) of farm women in this investigation were in medium category showing their own rationality while taking decisions followed by low (40.6%) and high (13.8%) categories with regard to rationality in decision making. Though farm women are endowed with ingenuity and diligence, they are shadowed by their husbands and family members in arriving at a rationality in decision making. Some farm women have proved that they were more rational in decision making as they always tried to achieve maximum return from their land holding, resources and in the existing farming system. The farm women could become more rational in decision making if they are allowed to be accessible to cosmopolite sources of information and consequently improve their farming performance.

Extension related variables

Extension contact : The pooled sample showed that 64.4 per cent of farm women were in the low category of extension contact, while 28.3 per cent belonged to medium category. This could be due to the fact that our agricultural extension system is mostly men oriented and hardly meets the needs of farm women. It has a very small per cent of women extension officers who can directly deal with farm women. Hence, it is desirable to have sufficient number of women extension functionaries and special programmes tailored to the needs of farm women to improve their extension contact and farming performance. Similar finding was also reported by Umadevi (1992).

Extension participation : Majority of farm women (66.1%) had low participation in extension activities followed by medium (27.8%) participation. The extension activities such as group meetings, farmer's days, demonstrations and skill trainings, etc. are mostly meant for men farmers leaving a very little chance for the farm women to participate. In our traditional society, it would not be practical to expect male extension agents to be able to motivate the farm women to participate in extension activities. The result was similar to that of Umadevi (1992).

Training : Out of the total respondents, 63.9 per cent of farm women belonged to low trained category followed by medium (27.7%) and high (8.4%) categories. Training is one of the means by which the desired changes in knowledge, skills and attitudes of farm women can be brought out. Therefore, the policy makers should provide training opportunities to the farm women in various aspects of crop and other allied enterprises to enhance their farming performance. The finding was in conformity of Sreedevi (1996).

Information seeking : In the present investigation, a majority of farm women (48.9%) were in the medium category followed by low (27.2%) and high (23.9%) categories in respect of information seeking in rice based farming practices. Mostly the farm women sought information from informal sources like family members, friends and relatives in the village. The cosmopolite and formal sources like women extension officers are to be inducted into our extension system who can directly deal with the farm needs of farm women which would undoubtedly accelerate the information seeking behaviour and consequently farm women become high information seekers.

Decision making pattern : The aggregate sample indicated that 60.6 per cent of farm women were placed in the medium category, while 23.3 per cent in high category in respect of decision making pattern related to farm and allied activities. This might be due to the fact that most of the husbands/head of the families of farm women shared information and also made them a party in the decision making on farm and allied activities. Nevertheless, the farm women are still kept away from taking important decisions like investments in inputs, selling and marketing of farm produce. The farm women could become the sole decision makers in the near future as there appears to be 'farm feminisation' taking place in rural areas. The result was in agreement with Shailaja (1990).

Role performance : Nearly half of the farm women (47.8%) in the sample were in the medium category and (40.5%) in the high category with regard to role performance in rice based farming activities. Since, farming was the main occupation and major source of income and coupled with labour shortage the farm women involved physically in most of the farm related operations on their own farms. The finding was in agreement with that of Bhuyan *et al.* (1988), Gosh *et al.* (1988) and Singh *et al.* (1988).

SECTION – B

ROLES PERFORMED BY DIFFERENT GROUPS OF FARM WOMEN IN RICE BASED FARMING SYSTEM

The data relating to the roles performed by different groups of farm women was analysed and the findings are presented under the following sub-heads:

Roles performed by large farm women in rice based farming system.
Roles performed by medium farm women in rice based farming system.
Roles performed by small farm women in rice based farming system.
Difference in roles performed by different groups of farm women.

Roles performed by large farm women in rice based farming system

Table 3 reveals how often the large farm women performed the identified roles in the rice based farming system (agriculture, horticulture and animal husbandry).

With regard to roles in agriculture, i.e., rice crop; the data in Table 3 indicates that majority of large farm women (60-68%) 'most often' performed the roles like 'drying the produce', 'storing the produce' and 'protection of stored produce'. More than 50 per cent of large farm women 'often' performed the roles like preparation of seed bed and winnowing. A great majority of large farm women (56-76 per cent) 'rarely' performed the roles like 'weeding in nursary', 'pulling and carrying seedlings to the main field', 'transplanting', 'gap filling in the main field,' 'weeding in the main field', 'harvesting of crop', etc.

In respect of horticulture, i.e., vegetable crops, the large farm women 'most often' performed roles like selection of vegetable crops and watering the nursery. Just 44 per cent of large farm women 'often' performed the roles like nursery bed preparation and spreading seed in the bed. A large majority (52-100%) of large farm women 'rarely' performed the roles like pulling and carrying seedlings to the main field, transplanting, weeding, scaring of birds, harvesting and preparation of vegetable products.

In case of animal husbandry, more than 50 per cent of large farm women 'often' performed the roles like milking, feeding

Table 3 : Roles performed by different groups of farm women in rice based farming systems

Sl. No.	Roles	Large (N = 25)						Medium (N = 65)						Small (N = 90)					
		Most often		Often		Rarely		Most often		Often		Rarely		Most often		Often		Rarely	
		F	%	F	%	F	%	F	%	F	%	F	%	F	%	F	%	F	%
	AGRICULTURE (RICE)																		
1.	Seed treatment	8	32.0	9	36.0	8	32.0	33	50.8	25	38.4	7	10.8	18	20.0	18	20.0	54	60.0
2.	Preparation of seed bed	4	16.0	13	52.0	8	32.0	30	46.2	20	30.8	15	23.0	90	100.0	—	—	—	—
3.	Seed soaking and spreading in the seed bed	6	24.0	8	32.0	11	44.0	60	92.3	5	7.7	—	—	90	100.0	—	—	—	—
4.	Weeding in nursery	2	8.0	5	20.0	18	72.0	55	84.6	10	15.4	—	—	72	80.0	18	20.0	—	—
5.	Pulling and carrying seedlings to the main field	6	24.0	5	20.0	14	56.0	45	69.2	10	15.4	10	15.4	10	15.4	90	100.0	—	—
6.	Transplanting	5	20.0	6	24.0	14	56.0	40	61.5	14	21.6	11	16.9	90	100.0	—	—	—	—
7.	Gap filling in the main field	4	16.0	7	20.0	14	56.0	40	61.5	18	27.7	7	10.8	90	100.0	—	—	—	—
8.	Weeding in the main field	3	12.0	3	12.0	19	76.0	35	53.8	14	21.6	16	24.6	90	100.0	—	—	—	—
9.	Harvesting of the crop	3	12.0	3	12.0	19	76.0	40	61.5	5	7.7	20	30.8	72	80.0	18	20.0	—	—
10.	Threshing	6	24.0	7	28.0	12	48.0	36	55.4	29	44.6	—	—	90	100.0	—	—	—	—
11.	Winnowing	10	.40.0	13	52.0	2	8.0	65	100.0	—	—	—	—	90	100.0	—	—	—	—
12.	Drying the produce	17	68.0	4	16.0	4	16.0	65	100.0	—	—	—	—	72	80.00	18	20.0	—	—
13.	Storing the produce	15	60.0	4	16.0	6	24.0	62	95.4	3	4.6	—	—	72	80.0	18	20.0	—	—
14.	Protection of stored produce	15	60.0	4	16.0	6	24.0	58	89.2	5	7.7	2	3.1	72	80.0	18	20.0	—	—

(Contd.)

Table 3 : *(Contd.)*

Sl. No.	Roles	Large (N = 25)						Medium (N = 65)						Small (N = 90)					
		Most often		Often		Rarely		Most often		Often		Rarely		Most often		Often		Rarely	
		F	%	F	%	F	%	F	%	F	%	F	%	F	%	F	%	F	%
HORTICULTURE (VEGETABLES)																			
1.	Selection of vegetable crop	14	56.0	7	28.0	4	16.0	27	41.5	20	30.8	18	27.7	66	73.3	24	26.7	—	—
2.	Nursery bed preparation	6	24.0	11	44.0	8	32.0	49	75.4	10	15.4	6	9.2	90	100.0	—	—	—	—
3.	Spreading seed in the bed	10	40.0	11	44.0	4	16.0	59	90.8	4	6.2	2	3.0	72	80.0	18	20.0	—	—
4.	Watering the nursery	14	56.0	6	24.0	5	20.0	64	98.5	—	—	1	1.5	72	80.0	18	20.0	—	—
5.	Pulling and carrying the seedling to the main field	2	8.0	10	40.0	13	52.0	53	81.5	12	18.5	—	—	90	100.0	—	—	—	—
6.	Transplanting	2	8.0	5	20.0	18	72.0	49	75.4	12	18.4	4	6.2	90	100.0	—	—	—	—
7.	Weeding in the main field	2	8.0	4	16.0	19	76.0	47	72.3	10	15.4	8	12.3	90	100.0	—	—	—	—
8.	Thinning or gap filling	6	24.0	9	36.0	10	40.0	57	87.7	8	12.3	—	—	80	100.0	—	—	—	—
9.	Scaring of birds	4	16.0	7	28.0	14	56.0	25	38.5	30	46.1	10	[illegible]	90	100.0	—	—	—	—
10.	Harvesting	2	8.0	2	8.0	21	84.0	51	78.4	4	6.2	10	16.4	87	96.7	3	3.3	—	—
11.	Preparation of vegetable products	—	—	—	—	25	100.0	—	—	4	6.2	61	93.8	—	—	—	—	90	100.0
ANIMAL HUSBANDRY (DAIRY/POULTRY)																			
1.	Milking	8	32.0	17	68.0	—	—	64	98.5	1	1.5	—	—	90	100.0	—	—	—	—
2.	Feeding animals	6	24.0	19	76.0	—	—	40	61.5	25	38.5	—	—	84	93.3	6	6.7	—	—

(Contd.)

Table 3 : *(Contd.)*

Sl. No.	Roles	Large (N = 25)						Medium (N = 65)						Small (N = 90)					
		Most often		Often		Rarely		Most often		Often		Rarely		Most often		Often		Rarely	
		F	%	F	%	F	%	F	%	F	%	F	%	F	%	F	%	F	%
3.	Maintenance of cattleshed	2	8.0	12	48.0	11	44.0	38	58.5	25	38.5	2	3.0	52	57.7	32	35.6	6	6.7
4.	Fodder collection	1	4.0	3	12.0	21	84.0	30	46.2	24	36.9	11	16.9	72	80.0	18	20.0	—	—
5.	Care & management of animals	2	8.0	13	52.0	10	40.0	40	61.5	25	38.5	—	—	78	86.7	12	13.3	—	—
6.	Marketing/disposal of milk	10	40.0	13	52.0	2	8.0	56	86.2	6	9.2	3	4.6	85	94.4	—	—	5	5.6
7.	Preparation of milk products	—	—	6	24.0	19	76.0	20	30.8	27	41.5	18	27.7	—	—	—	—	90	100.0
8.	Preparation of cowdung cakes for fuel	—	—	—	—	25	100.0	10	16.4	30	46.2	25	38.4	45	50.0	39	43.3	6	6.7
9.	Feeding the poultry birds	—	—	2	8.0	23	92.0	3	4.6	46	70.8	16	24.6	35	38.9	39	43.3	16	17.8
10.	Maintenance of bird cages	—	—	4	16.0	21	84.0	—	—	-	—	65	100.0	—	—	—	—	90	100.0
11.	Collection of eggs	6	24.0	19	76.0	—	—	20	30.8	45	69.2	—	—	21	23.3	69	76.7	—	—
12.	Selection of eggs for hatching	8	32.0	12	48.0	5	20.0	3	4.6	62	95.4	—	—	20	22.2	70	77.8	—	—
13.	Caring of sick birds	6	24.0	8	32.0	11	44.0	—	—	6	9.2	59	90.8	—	—	60	66.7	30	33.3

animals, care and management of animals, marketing of milk and collection of eggs. A great majority (76-92 per cent) of large farm women 'rarely' performed roles like fodder collection, preparation of milk products, preparation of cowdung cakes as fuel, feeding poultry birds and maintenance of bird cages, etc.

This might be due to the fact that land owning large farm women do not most often physically work on their farms by themselves. As the farm size increased, work participation of farm women decreased in the farm sector and increased in dairy sector. Large farm women feel below to their dignity and prestige to work in the fields. However, most of the post-harvest operations and dairy activities are done within the homesteads and that was the reason why their participation was more in post-harvest operations and animal husbandry enterprise.

Role performed by medium farm women in rice based farming system

Table 3 indicates the pattern of role performance of medium farm women in rice based farming system.

With respect to role performance in agriculture, i.e., rice crop, the table shows that a large majority (50-100%) of medium farm women 'most often' performed the roles like seed treatment, seed soaking and spreading in seed bed, weeding in nursery, pulling and carrying seedlings to the main field, transplanting, gap filling in the main field, weeding in the main field, harvesting of the crop, threshing, winnowing, drying and storing the produce and protection of stored produce.

In case of horticulture, i.e., vegetable crops, the data reveals that majority (72-98 per cent) of medium farm women 'most often' performed the roles such as nursery bed preparation, spreading seed in the bed, watering the nursary, pulling and carrying seedlings to the main field, transplanting, weeding, thinning and gap filling and harvesting. Medium farm women 'rarely' performed the role of preparation of vegetable products.

Under identified roles in animal husbandry, more than 60 per cent of medium farm women 'most often' performed roles such as milking, feeding animals, maintenance of cattle shed, care and management of animals, marketing of milk, etc., 70 per cent of respondents 'often' performed roles like feeding poultry birds, collection of eggs, selection of eggs for hatching. Ninety per cent of medium farm women 'rarely' involved in the role of maintenance of bird cages and caring of sick birds.

The medium farm women do engage agricultural labour to work in their farms and at the same time they also involve physically in most of the field operations along with the labour. These groups of farm women do not feel below dignity or prestige to work in their fields. Moreover, the medium farm women have no other way except to depend on agriculture and farm related activities which are major sources of their income. These women can neither afford to waste time like large farm women nor go in for non-agricultural activities (like working as agricultural labour in other farms, vegetable vendors etc.) like small farm women. This group of farm women also performed most of the animal husbandry operations as this was another major source of income. These might be the plausible reasons for the better role performance of medium farm women in rice based farming system.

Roles performed by small farm women in rice based farming system

Table 3 reveals the role performance of small farm women in rice based farming system.

In respect of agriculture, i.e., rice crop, majority of small farm women 'most often' performed the roles such as preparation of seed bed (100%), seed soaking and spreading in the seed bed (100%), weeding in nursery (80%), pulling and carrying seedlings to the main field (100%), transplanting (100%), gap filling in the main field (100%), weeding in the main field (100%), harvesting (80%), threshing (100%), winnowing (100%), drying the produce (80%), storing the produce (80%) and protection of stored produce (80%), and 60 per cent of small farm women 'rarely' performed the role like seed treatment.

With regard to horticulture, i.e., vegetable crops, most of the small farm women 'most often' involved in the roles such as selection of vegetable crops (73.3%), nursary bed preparation (100%), spreading seed in the bed (80%), watering the nursery (80%), pulling and carrying seedlings to the main field (100%), transplanting (100%), weeding (100%), thinning and gap filling (100%), scaring of birds (100%) and harvesting (96.7%). Small farm women 'rarely' performed the role like 'preparation of vegetable products'.

Under animal husbandry, the small farm women 'most often' performed roles such as milking (100%), feeding animals (93.3%), maintenance of cattle shed (57.7%), fodder collection (80%), care and management of animals (86.7%), marketing of milk (94.4%), preparation of cowdung cakes for fuel (50.0%). They were also 'often' involved in collection of eggs, selection of eggs for hatching and caring of sick birds. Small farm women 'rarely' involved in the preparation of milk products.

The small farm women generally belonged to low income group and the income obtained from small holding may not be sufficient for a reasonably comfortable living and so they cannot afford to engage hired labour to work in their fields. These women work in their fields and perform all the roles involving physical work. Sometimes, they also work in other farms as hired labour to augment the family income. Almost all the roles identified under animal husbandry were performed by this group of farm women because of their low economic base. The dairy enterprise provide an additional substantial source of income and so their participation was more in this enterprise too.

In the light of the above discussion, the general impression that women do not perform all the roles identified under agriculture, horticulture and animal husbandry cannot be agreed. Hence, it can be concluded that the role of farm women of all groups in present day agriculture and related enterprises is inevitable in sustaining the productivity and production.

Difference in roles performed by different groups of farm women

F-test was employed to find out any significant difference in role performance among the three groups of farm women in rice based farming system. Difference in role performance among the three groups of farm women :

N.H. : There will be no significant difference in the scores of role performance among three groups of farm women.

E.H. : There will be significant difference in the scores of role performance among three groups of farm women.

Since the overall F-ratio value(10.9703) was greater than the table value of 'F' with respect to the corresponding degrees of freedom, the null hypothesis was rejected at 0.01 level of probability (Table 4).

Table 4 : Difference in role performance among three groups of farm women

Source of Variation	DF	Sum of squares	Mean squares	F-ratio
Groups	2	4019.3750	2009.6875	10.9703**
Error	177	32435.2500	183.1935	
Total	179	36444.6250		

** Significant at 0.01 level of probability.

Hence, it can be concluded that there was significant difference among the scores of three groups of farm women in respect of role performance.

To confirm which group means differed significantly, the mean scores of three groups were arranged in descending order of magnitude with the corresponding critical differences and compared as shown below :

	Medium	Small	Large
Means	83.85	82.79	69.64
C.D.	5.99	4.32	6.24

Thus, mean scores of role performance between medium and small farm women do not differ significantly which was indicated by a bar. Therefore, it can be concluded that there was significant difference in the mean scores of large and medium, and large and small farm women in respect of role performance in rice based farming system. In other words, the medium farm women had the highest mean scores, i.e., 83.85 followed closely by small farm women (82.79).The large farm women had the lowest mean score, i.e., 69.64 in respect of role performance.(Figure 3)

The above findings were in the expected direction. The medium and small farm women had to depend on the income generated from farm and related enterprises and hence, they physically perform all the roles as they cannot afford to engage hired labour as it is scarce and expensive and adds to the cost of cultivation, whereas the large farm women who are economically well off could engage hired labour for different operations and hence, they did not participate or perform the roles which required physical or muscle energy. This could be the probable reason for the significant difference between large, medium and small groups of farm women in their role performance in rice based farming system. Similar findings were reported by Shailaja (1990).

SECTION – C

ROLE PERCEPTION OF DIFFERENT GROUPS OF FARM WOMEN AND THEIR HUSBANDS IN SELECTED ENTERPRISES IN RICE BASED FARMING SYSTEM

Role perception is conceptualised as the reaction of farm women and their husbands towards the expected roles of farm women as 'most important', 'important' and 'least important' in a rice based farming system. The rice based farming system in this study includes the selected enterprises such as agriculture (rice), horticulture (vegetable crops) and animal husbandry (dairy/poultry)

The results relating to this aspect are presented in the following sub-heads:

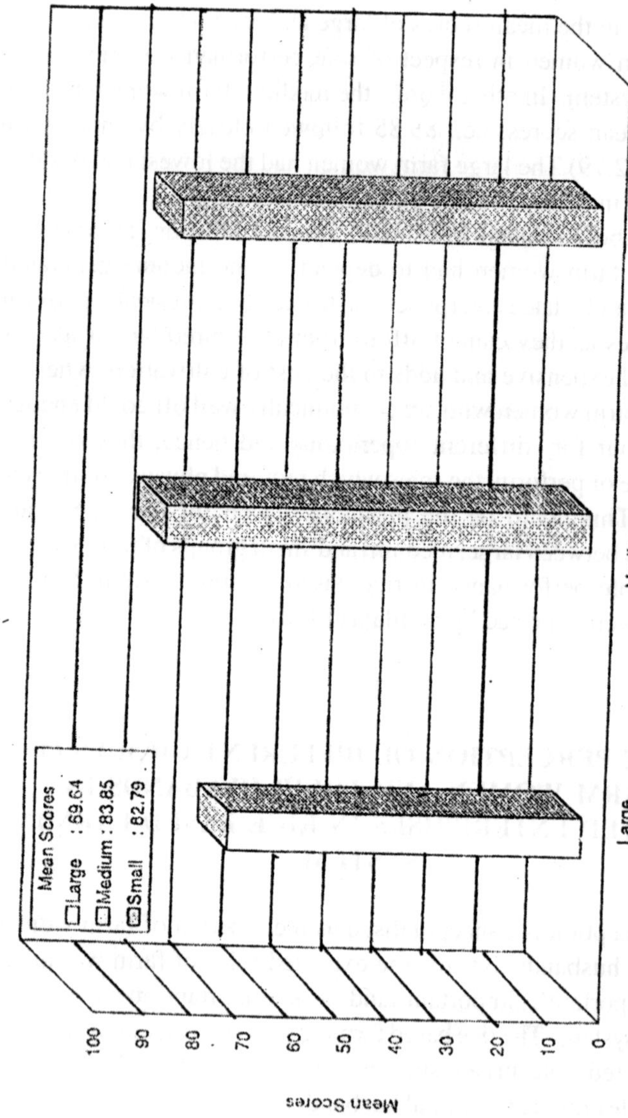

Fig 3 : Roles performed by different groups of farm women.

Role perception of large farm women and their husbands.
Role perception of medium farm women and their husbands.
Role perception of small farm women and their husbands.

Role perception of large farm women and their husbands

Item analysis was carried out to find out the perception of farm women and their husbands in selected enterprises of rice based farming system. The results obtained are presented below :

It may be observed from Table 5 that large farm women perceived their role in rice cultivation as 'most important' in respect of 'seed treatment' (56.0%), 'gap filling in the main field' (60.0%), winnowing (60.0%), 'drying the produce' (60.0%), 'storing the produce' (80.0%) and 'protection of stored produce' (76.0%). Their husbands perceived only three roles as 'most important', viz., 'drying the produce (56.0%), 'storing the produce' (84.0%), and 'protection of stored produce' (76.0%).

Most of the large farm women and their husbands perceived 'least important' the roles such as 'preparation of seed bed', 'seed soaking and spreading in the seed bed', 'weeding in the nursary', 'pulling and carrying seedlings to the main field', 'transplanting', 'weeding in the main field', 'harvesting of the crop', and 'threshing'.

With regard to horticulture (vegetable crops), the large farm women perceived 'most important', the roles such as 'selection of vegetable crops' (56%), 'spreading seed in the bed' (84%), 'watering the nursery' (76%), and 'preparation of vegetable produces' (60%). Their husbands perceived only three roles such as 'spreading seed in the bed' (80%), 'watering the nursery' (60%), and 'preparation of vegetable produces' (72%) as 'most important'.

Both large farm women and their husbands perceived as 'least important', roles such as 'nursery bed preparation', 'pulling and carrying seedlings to the main field', 'transplanting', 'weeding in the main field', 'thinning or gap filling', 'scaring of birds' and 'harvesting'.

In respect of animal husbandry (dairy/poultry), the large farm women perceived 'most important' the roles like 'milking' (76%), 'feeding animals' (52%), 'marketing/disposal of milk' (80%),

Table 5 : Role perception of large farm women and their husbands

Sl. No.	Roles	Farm women (N = 25)			Husbands (N = 25)		
		Most impor-tant	Impor-tant	Least impor-tant	Most impor-tant	Impor-tant	Least impor-tant
	AGRICULTURE (RICE)						
1.	Seed treatment	14	11	—	6	19	—
		(56.0)	(44.0)	—	(24.0)	(76.0)	—
2.	Preparation of seed	—	5	20	—	—	25
	bed	—	(20.0)	(80.0)	—	—	(100.0)
3.	Seed soaking and	—	4	21	—	5	20
	spreading in the seed bed	—	(16.0)	(84.0)	—	(20.0)	(80.0)
4.	Weeding in nursary	—	4	21	—	4	21
		—	(16.0)	(84.0)	—	(16.0)	(84.0)
5.	Pulling & carrying seed-	—	4	21	—	4	21
	lings to the main field	—	(16.0)	(84.0)	—	(16.0)	(84.0)
6.	Transplanting	4	5	16	—	6	19
		(16.0)	(20.0)	(64.0)	—	(24.0)	(76.0)
7.	Gap filling in the	—	15	10	—	14	11
	main field	—	(60.0)	(40.0)	—	(56.0)	(44.0)
8.	Weeding in the main	—	8	17	—	4	21
	field	—	(32.0)	(68.0)	—	(16.0)	(84.0)
9.	Harvesting of the crop	—	5	20	—	4	21
		—	(20.00)	(80.00)	—	(16.0)	(84.0)
10.	Threshing	—	8	17	—	5	20
		—	(32.0)	(68.0)	—	(20.00)	(80.0)
11.	Winnowing	—	15	10	—	7	18
		—	(60.00)	(40.0)	—	(28.0)	(72.0)
12.	Drying the produce	15	10	—	14	11	—
		(60.0)	(40.0)	—	(56.0)	(44.0)	—
13.	Storing the produce	20	5	—	21	4	—
		(80.0)	(20.0)	—	(84.0)	(16.0)	—
14.	Protection of stored	19	6	—	19	6	—
	produce	(76.0)	(24.0)	—	(76.0)	(24.0)	—

(Contd.)

Table 5 : *(Contd.)*

Sl. No.	Roles	Farm women (N = 25)			Husbands (N = 25)		
		Most impor-tant	Impor-tant	Least impor-tant	Most impor-tant	Impor-tant	Least impor-tant
	HORTICULTURE (VEGETABLES)						
1.	Selection of vegetable crop	14 (56.0)	11 (44.0)	— —	8 (32.0)	17 (68.0)	— —
2.	Nursery bed prepara-tion	— —	6 (24.0)	19 (76.0)	— —	4 (16.0)	21 (84.00)
3.	Spreading seed in the bed	21 (84.0)	4 (16.0)	— —	20 (80.0)	5 (20.0)	— —
4.	Watering the nursary	19 (76.0)	6 (24.0)	— —	15 (60.0)	10 (40.0)	— —
5.	Pulling and carrying the seedlings to the main field	— —	8 (32.0)	17 (68.0)	— —	5 (20.0)	20 (80.0)
6.	Transplanting	— —	8 (32.0)	17 (68.0)	— —	4 (16.0)	21 (84.0)
7.	Weeding in the main field	— —	9 (36.0)	16 (64.0)	— —	4 (16.00)	21 (84.0)
8.	Thinning or gap filling	— —	7 (28.0)	18 (72.0)	— —	5 (20.0)	20 (80.0)
9.	Scaring of birds	— —	6 (24.0)	19 (76.0)	— —	7 (28.0)	18 (72.0)
10.	Harvesting	5 (20.0)	10 (40.0)	10 (40.0)	— —	4 (16.0)	21 (84.0)
11.	Preparation of vege-table products	15 (60.00)	10 (40.0)	— —	18 (72.00	7 (28.0)	— —
	ANIMAL HUSBANDRY (DAIRY/POULTRY)						
1.	Milking	19 (76.0)	6 (24.0)	— —	15 (60.0)	10 (40.0)	— —
2.	Feeding animals	13 (52.0)	12 (48.0)	— —	10 (40.0)	15 (60.0)	— —

(Contd.)

Table 5 : *(Contd.)*

Sl. No.	Roles	Farm women (N = 25)			Husbands (N = 25)		
		Most Impor-tant	Impor-tant	Least impor-tant	Most impor-tant	Impor-tant	Least impor-tant
3.	Maintenance of cattleshed	—	7	18	—	5	20
		—	(28.0)	(72.0)	—	(20.0)	(80.0)
4.	Fodder collection	—	—	25	—	—	25
		—	—	(100.0)	—	—	(100.00)
5.	Care & management of animals	10	15	—	15	10	—
		(40.0)	(60.0)	—	(60.0)	(40.0)	—
6.	Marketing/disposal of milk	20	5	—	25	—	—
		(80.0)	(20.0)	—	(100.0)	—	—
7.	Preparation of milk products	21	4	—	25	—	—
		(84.0)	(16.0)	—	(100.0)	—	—
8.	Preparation of cow-dung cakes for fuel	—	—	25	—	—	25
		—	—	(100.0)	—	—	(100.0)
9.	Feeding the poultry birds	15	10	—	14	11	—
		(60.0)	(40.0)	—	(56.0)	(44.0)	—
10.	Maintenance of birds cages	15	10	—	10	15	—
		(60.0)	(40.0)	—	(40.0)	(60.0)	—
11.	Collection of eggs	20	5	—	25	—	—
		(80.0)	(20.00)	—	(100.0)	—	—
12.	Selection of eggs for hatching	21	4	—	25	—	—
		(84.0)	(16.0)	—	(100.0)	—	—
13.	Caring of sick birds	25	—	—	25	—	—
		(100.0)	—	—	(100.0)	—	—

Note : Figures in parentheses indicate percentages.

'preparation of milk produces' (84%), 'feeding the poultry birds' (60%), 'maintenance of bird cages' (60%), 'collection of eggs' (80%), 'selection of eggs for hatching' (84%), and 'caring of sick birds' (100%). Same roles were perceived by their husbands as most important.

Both large farm women and their husbands perceived 'least important' roles such as 'maintenance of cattleshed', 'fodder collection', 'preparation of cow dung cakes for fuel'.

The large farm women and their husbands perceived limited roles in agriculture and horticulture and most of the identified roles in animal husbandry enterprises as most important as they did not differ in their role perception. The plausible reason for this might be that both of them felt that the roles which involved physical work are not their jobs because of their higher social and economic status. They also felt that it is below to their dignity and prestige to go to the fields which are far off from their homes to perform the field operations. Moreover, these women do not possess strong physical body to undertake field operations involving drudgery. Since large farm women who are mostly confined to their homes have shown positive perception to undertake most of the identified animal husbandry roles as these roles do not require much physical energy and can be performed in the homesteads. The large farm women attend to cattle everyday which starts with milking, then attends to the kitchen where milk is boiled. Some- times milk products like butter milk and butter are made. The milk is sold in the village itself through milk collection centres. She also feeds the animals with balanced nutrition etc. The social norms related to the management and care of the livestock on large family farms are such that most of the work related to animal husbandry are allotted to women only.

Difference in role perception of selected enterprises between large farm women and their husbands

Data relating to the perception of large farm women and their husbands were analysed by applying 'z' test to find out the difference in their perception. The results are presented in Table 6.

It is evident from Table 6, based on the computed 'Z' values, the large farm women did not significantly differ with their husbands in respect of role perception in the selected enterprises of rice based farming system.

Table 6: Difference in role perception of selected enterprises between large farm women and their husbands

Sl. No.	Selected enterprises	Large farm women		Husbands		Calculated 'Z' value
		Mean	SD	Mean	SD	
1.	Agriculture (rice)	31.52	4.59	30.08	4.66	1.10NS
2.	Horticulture	26.72	3.26	25.52	3.08	1.33NS
3.	Animal husbandry	33.60	3.25	32.92	3.40	0.69NS

NS = Non-significant.

Role perception of medium farm women and their husbands

The data presented in Table 7 reveal the perception of medium farm women and their husbands about the expected roles in the selected enterprises.

It can be observed from Table 7 that medium farm women perceived their roles in rice cultivation as 'most important' in respect of 'seed soaking and spreading in the seed bed' (69.2%), 'weeding in the nursery' (77%), 'gap filling in the main field' (100%), 'threshing' (61.5%), 'winnowing' (69.2%), 'drying the produce, (100%), 'storing the produce' (100%), and 'protection of stored produce' (100%). Their husbands also perceived 'most important' the roles such as 'seed soaking and spreading in the seed bed' (61.5%), 'weeding in the nursery' (84.6%), 'gap filling in the main field' (100%), 'threshing' (53.8%), 'winnowing' (61.5%), 'drying the produce' (100%), 'storing the produce' (100%), and 'protection of stored produce' (100%).

Most of the medium farm women and their husbands perceived 'least important' the roles such as 'preparation of seed bed', and 'pulling and carrying seedlings to the main field'.

Table 7 : Role perception of medium farm women and their husbands

Sl. No.	Roles	Farm women (N=65)			Husbands (N=65)		
		Most impor-tant	impor-tant	Least impor-tant	Most impor-tant	Impor-tant	Least impor-tant
	AGRICULTURE (RICE)						
1.	Seed treatment	15	25	25	—	40	25
		(23.0)	(38.5)	(38.5)	—	(61.5)	(38.5)
2.	Preparation of seed	10	20	35	—	20	45
	bed	(15.4)	(30.8)	(53.8)	—	(30.8)	(69.2)
3.	Seed soaking & sprea-	45	20	—	40	25	—
	ding in the seed bed	(69.2)	(30.8)	—	(61.5)	(38.5)	—
4.	Weeding in nursery	50	15	—	55	10	—
		(77.0)	(23.0)	—	(84.6)	(15.4)	—
5.	Pulling & carrying seed-	—	20	45	—	15	50
	lings to the main field	—	(30.8)	(69.2)	—	(23.0)	(77.0)
6.	Transplanting	25	40	—	20	45	—
		(38.5)	(61.5)	—	(38.8)	(69.2)	—
7.	Gap filling in the	65	—	—	65	—	—
	main field	(100.0)	—	—	(100.0)	—	—
8.	Weeding in the main	25	40	—	20	45	—
	field	(38.5)	(61.5)	—	(30.8)	(69.2)	—
9.	Harvesting of the crop	30	35	—	25	40	—
		(46.2)	(53.8)	—	(38.5)	(61.5)	—
10.	Threshing	40	25	—	35	30	—
		(61.5)	(38.5)	—	(61.5)	(38.5)	—
11.	Winnowing	45	20	—	40	25	—
		(69.2)	(30.8)	—	(61.5)	(38.5)	—
12.	Drying the produce	65	—	—	65	—	—
		(100.0)	—	—	(100.0)	—	—
13.	Storing the produce	65	—	—	65	—	—
		(100.0)	—	—	(100.0)	—	—
14.	Protection of stored	65	—	—	65	—	—
	produce	(100.0)	—	—	(100.0)	—	—

(Contd.)

Table 7 : *(Contd.)*

Sl. No.	Roles	Farm women (N = 65)			Husbands (N = 65)		
		Most impor-tant	impor-tant	Least impor-tant	Most impor-tant	Impor-tant	Least impor-tant
HORTICULTURE (VEGETABLES)							
1.	Selection of vegetable crop	20 (30.8)	30 (46.2)	15 (23.00)	— —	25 (38.5)	40 (61.5)
2.	Nursery bed preparation	35 (53.8)	30 (46.2)	— —	30 (46.2)	35 (53.8)	— —
3.	Spreading seed in the bed	45 (69.2)	20 (30.8)	— —	50 (77.0)	15 (23.0)	— —
4.	Watering the nursery	65 (100.0)	— —	— —	65 (100.0)	— —	— —
5.	Pulling and carrying the seedlings to the main field	— —	25 (38.5)	40 (61.5)	— —	15 (23.0)	50 (77.0)
6.	Transplanting	25 (38.5)	40 (61.5)	— —	15 (23.0)	50 (77.0)	— —
7.	Weeding in the main field	15 (23.0)	25 (38.5)	25 (38.5)	— —	25 (38.5)	40 (61.5)
8.	Thinning or gap filling	50 (77.0)	15 (23.0)	— —	45 (69.2)	20 (30.8)	— —
9.	Scaring of birds	— —	25 (38.5)	40 (61.5)	— —	20 (30.8)	45 (69.2)
10.	Harvesting	40 (61.5)	25 (38.5)	— —	35 (53.8)	30 (46.2)	— —
11.	Preparation of vegetable products	39 (60.0)	26 (40.0)	— —	49 (75.4)	16 (24.6)	— —
ANIMAL HUSBANDRY (DAIRY/POULTRY)							
1.	Milking	48 (73.8)	17 (26.2)	— —	50 (77.0)	15 (23.0)	— —
2.	Feeding animals	50 (77.0)	15 (23.0)	— —	45 (69.2)	20 (30.8)	— —

(Contd.)

Table 7 : *(Contd.)*

No.		Farm women (N = 65) Most important	Farm women Important	Farm women Least important	Husbands (N = 65) Most important	Husbands Important	Husbands Least important
3.	Maintenance of cattleshed	15	25	25	—	35	30
		(23.0)	(38.5)	(38.5)	—	(53.8)	(46.2)
4.	Fodder collection	—	20	45	—	15	50
		—	(30.8)	(69.2)	—	(23.0)	(77.0)
5.	Care & management of animals	47	18	—	50	15	—
		(72.3)	(27.7)	—	(77.0)	(23.0)	—
6.	Marketing/disposal of milk	65	—	—	65	—	—
		(100.0)	—	—	(100.0)	—	—
7.	Preparation of milk products	46	19	—	52	13	—
		(70.8)	(29.2)	—	(80.0)	(20.0)	—
8.	Preparation of cow-dung cakes for fuel	—	20	45	—	10	55
		—	(30.8)	(69.2)	—	(15.4)	(84.6)
9.	Feeding the poultry birds	50	15	—	65	—	—
		(77.0)	(23.0)	—	(100.0)	—	—
10.	Maintenance of birds cages	65	—	—	65	—	—
		(100.0)	—	—	(100.0)	—	—
11.	Collection of eggs	65	—	—	65	—	—
		(100.0)	—	—	(100.0)	—	—
12.	Selection of eggs for hatching	25	25	15	35	30	—
		(38.5)	(38.5)	(23.0)	(53.8)	(46.2)	—
13.	Caring of sick birds	35	30	—	48	17	—
		(53.8)	(46.2)	—	(73.8)	(26.2)	—

Note : Figures in parentheses indicate percentages.

In case of horticultural crops, the medium farm women perceived 'most important' the roles like 'nursery bed preparation' (53.8%), 'spreading seed in the bed' (69.2%), 'watering the nursery' (100%), 'thinning and gap filling in the main field' (77%), and 'preparation of vegetable products' (60%). Their husbands perceived the 'most important', the roles such as 'spreading seed in the bed' (77%), 'watering the nursery' (100%), 'thinning or gap filling' (69.2%), 'harvesting' (53.8%) and 'preparation of vegetable products (75.4%).

Both medium farm women and their husbands perceived as 'least important', the roles like 'pulling and carrying seedlings to the main field', 'weeding in the main field', and 'scaring of birds'.

With regard to animal husbandry, majority of medium farm women and their husbands perceived as 'most important', the roles such as milking', 'feeding the animals', 'care and management of animals', 'marketing/disposal of milk', 'preparation of milk products', 'feeding the poultry birds', 'maintenance of bird cages', 'collection of eggs', and 'caring of sick birds'.

Majority of medium farm women and their husbands perceived 'least important' the roles like 'fodder collection', 'maintenance of cattleshed', and 'preparation of cowdung cakes for fuel'.

Table 8 : Difference in role perception of selected enterprises between medium farm women and their husbands

Sl. No.	Selected enterprises	Medium farm women		Husbands		Calculated 'Z' value
		Mean	SD	Mean	SD	
1.	Agriculture (rice)	36.11	3.01	33.68	3.04	4.58**
2.	Horticulture	27.25	3.46	26.31	3.31	1.59NS
3.	Animal husbandry	33.20	2.81	31.83	3.56	1.45NS

** Significant at 0.01 level of probability.
NS = Non-significant

It is evident from Table 8 that based on 'Z' values, medium farm women did not differing with their husbands in role perception in horticulture and animal husbandry enterprises. However, the difference in perception of medium farm women and their husbands was found significant in agriculture enterprise.

The 'Z' test with regard to their role perception revealed that the medium farm women did not differ with their husbands in role perception with respect to horticulture and animal husbandry enterprises but differ significantly in agriculture. The probable reason for the significant difference in agriculture might be due to the fact that middle class women are prepared to take up roles like transplanting, weedings and harvesting involving lot of drudgery and physical energy with a view to avoid hired labour and reduce the cost of cultivation. But the husbands do not share this view as they are society conscious and fear to break the existing social taboos and customs relating to women folk.

Role perception of small farm women and their husbands

The data presented in Table 9 indicate the perception of small farm women and their husbands about the expected roles in the selected enterprises.

It may be seen from Table 9 that majority of small farm women and their husbands (i.e., 70-100%) perceived their roles in rice cultivation as 'most important' in case of 'preparation of seed bed', 'seed soaking and spreading in the bed', 'weeding in the nursery', 'pulling and carrying seedlings to the main field', 'transplanting', 'gap filling in the main field', 'weeding in the main field', 'harvesting of the crop', 'threshing, 'winnowing', 'drying the produce', 'storing the produce', and 'protection of stored produce'.

Majority (50%) of small farm women and their husbands perceived 'least important', the only role', i.e., 'seed treatment'.

In case of horticultural crops, majority of small farm women and their husbands (100%) perceived all the identified roles as 'most important' except two roles, i.e., 'scaring of birds' and 'preparation of vegetable products' which they termed as 'least important'.

With respect to animal husbandry, almost all (100%) the small farm women and their husbands perceived 'most important' all the identified roles except 'preparation of milk products' which they termed as 'least important'.

It is evident from Table 10 that based on 'Z' values, small farm women did not significantly differ with their husbands in respect of role perception in the selected enterprises, viz., agriculture, horticulture and animal husbandry.

The 'Z' test results revealed that small farm women did not differ significantly with their husbands in respect of role perception in the selected enterprises of rice based farming system.

Medium and small farm women and their husbands continue

Table 9 : Role perception of small farm women and their husbands

Sl. No.	Roles	Farm women (N = 90)			Husbands (N = 90)		
		Most impor- tant	Impor- tant	Least impor- tant	Most impor- tant	Impor- tant	Least impor- tant
AGRICULTURE (RICE)							
1.	Seed treatment	15 (16.7)	25 (27.8)	50 (55.5)	20 (22.2)	25 (27.8)	45 (50.0)
2.	Preparation of seed bed	63 (70.0)	27 (30.0)	— —	60 (66.7)	30 (33.3)	— —
3.	Seed soaking & spreading in the seed bed	90 (100.0)	— —	— —	90 (100.0)	— —	— —
4.	Weeding in nursary	90 (100.0)	— —	— —	90 (100.0)	— —	— —
5.	Pulling & carrying seedlings to the main field	90 (100.0)	— —	— —	90 (100.0)	— —	— —
6.	Transplanting	90 (100.0)	— —	— —	90 (100.0)	— —	— —
7.	Gap filling in the main field	90 (100.0)	— —	— —	90 (100.0)	— —	— —
8.	Weeding in the main field	90 (100.0)	— —	— —	90 (100.0)	— —	— —
9.	Crop Harvesting of the	90 (100.0)	— —	— —	90 (100.0)	— —	— —
10.	Threshing	90 (100.0)	— —	— —	90 (100.0)	— —	— —
11.	Winnowing	90 (100.0)	— —	— —	90 (100.0)	— —	— —
12.	Drying the produce	80 (88.9)	10 (11.1)	— —	90 (100.0)	— —	— —
13.	Storing the produce	90 (100.0)	— —	— —	90 (100.0)	— —	— —
14.	Protection of stored produce	90 (100.0)	— —	— —	90 (100.0)	— —	— —

(Contd.)

Table 9 : *(Contd.)*

Sl. No.	Roles	Farm women (N = 90)			Husbands (N = 90)		
		Most important	Important	Least important	Most important	Important	Least important
	HORTICULTURE (VEGETABLES)						
1.	Selection of vegetable crop	50 (55.5)	40 (44.5)	— —	30 (33.3)	40 (44.5)	20 (22.2)
2.	Nursery bed preparation	90 (100.0)	— —	— —	90 (100.0)	— —	— —
3.	Spreading seed in the bed	90 (100.0)	— —	— —	90 (100.0)	— —	— —
4.	Watering the nursary	90 (100.0)	— —	— —	90 (100.0)	— —	— —
5.	Pulling and carrying the seedlings to the main field	90 (100.0)	— —	— —	90 (100.0)	— —	— —
6.	Transplanting	90 (100.0)	— —	— —	90 (100.0)	— —	— —
7.	Weeding in the main field	90 (100.0)	— —	— —	90 (100.0)	— —	— —
8.	Thinning or gap filling	90 (100.0)	— —	— —	90 (100.0)	— —	— —
9.	Scaring of birds	40 (44.5)	20 (22.2)	30 (33.3)	30 (33.3)	20 (22.2)	40 (44.5)
10.	Harvesting	90 (100.0)	— —	— —	90 (100.0)	— —	— —
11.	Preparation of vegetable products	15 (16.7)	25 (27.8)	50 (55.5)	— —	20 (22.2)	70 (77.8)
	ANIMAL HUSBANDRY (DAIRY/POULTRY)						
1.	Milking	90 (100.0)	— —	— —	90 (100.0)	— —	— —
2.	Feeding animals	90 (100.0)	— —	— —	90 (100.0)	— —	— —

(Contd.)

Table 9 : *(Contd.)*

Sl. No.	Roles	Farm women (N = 90)			Husbands (N = 90)		
		Most impor-tant	Impor-tant	Least impor-tant	Most impor-tant	Impor-tant	Least impor-tant
3.	Maintainance of cattleshed	90 (100.0)	—	—	90 (100.0)	—	—
4.	Fodder collection	90 (100.0)	—	—	90 (100.0)	—	—
5.	Care & management of animals	50 (55.5)	40 (44.5)	—	40 (44.5)	50 (55.5)	—
6.	Marketing/disposal of milk	90 (100.0)	—	—	90 (100.0)	—	—
7.	Preparation of milk products	—	20 (22.2)	70 (77.8)	—	15 (16.7)	75 (83.3)
8.	Preparation of cow-dung cakes for fuel	90 (100.0)	—	—	90 (100.0)	—	—
9.	Feeding the poultry birds	90 (100.0)	—	—	90 (100.0)	—	—
10.	Maintenance of birds cages	90 (100.0)	—	—	90 (100.0)	—	—
11.	Collection of eggs	90 (100.0)	—	—	90 (100.0)	—	—
12.	Selection of eggs for hatching	90 (100.0)	—	—	90 (100.0)	—	—
13.	Caring of sick birds	90 (100.0)	—	—	90 (100.0)	—	—

Note : Figures in parentheses indicate percentage.

to perceive their roles in agriculture, horticulture and animal husbandry activities as most important as feminisation of agriculture is beginning to take place. Small farm women's husbands generally chose employment outside their villages and women are left behind to look after agriculture and related activities. This has made the small farm women's participation more and hence, more perception.The more number of medium and small farm women had positive perception because of differentiations in size of holding,

Table 10 : Difference in role perception of selected enterprises between small farm women and their husbands

Sl. No.	Selected enterprises	Small farm women		Husbands		Calculated 'Z' value
		Mean	S.D.	Mean	S.D.	
1.	Agriculture (rice)	36.90	3.28	36.48	3.24	0.81NS
2.	Horticulture	25.68	4.18	24.77	4.77	1.38NS
3.	Animal husbandry	34.63	3.55	34.77	3.61	0.26NS

NS = Non-significant.

economic status which are widely prevalent in rural areas. The peculiarity of the agrarian structure in Andhra Pradesh is such that there is a large mass of self-cultivating peasant farmers constituting its backbone and hence, most of them have become medium and small owner cultivators and forcing them to involve in all the roles physically and the same was perceived by them.

In case of animal husbandry which is an important aspect of every farm household particularly medium and small farm families since it makes a substantial contribution to the family subsistence needs. Therefore, tending of livestock for the farm families is an income generating activity and cannot be treated as having merely use-value and that is why medium and small farm women and their husbands perceived all most all the identified roles as 'most important'.

SECTION – D

AREAS AND DECISION MAKING PATTERN OF FARM WOMEN IN RICE BASED FARMING SYSTEM

Twenty decision making areas were identified in rice based farming system after duly consulting the experts and field extension officers wherein farm women can take decisions on their own or in consultation with their husband/head of the families, neighbours, relatives and friends. The data thus obtained on the decision making pattern of farm women was analysed and presented in the following sub-heads:

Decision making pattern of large farm women.
Decision making pattern of medium farm women.
Decision making pattern of small farm women.
Difference in decision making pattern among three groups of farm women.

Areas and decision making pattern of large farm women

The data in Table 11 revealed that majority of large farm women (68-100%) took decisions 'by themselves' in case of use of family labour, selling of milk and milk products, health management of poultry and selling of eggs and birds.

While more than 50 per cent of large farm women were involved in taking decisions in consultation with their husbands/head of the families with regard to number of animals to be maintained, quantity of feed to be given to milch and other animals and spending income from farm enterprises.

In large farm women families most of the decisions, viz., choice of crops/enterprises, selection of seeds, storage of produce, selling of surplus farm produce, quantity of grain/vegetables to be disposed, sale and purchase of draught animals and artificial insemination to animals were 'exclusively taken by their husbands/heads of the families'.

Areas and decision making pattern of medium farm women

A perusal of Table 11 indicates the pattern of decision making in medium farm women families. These farm women took decisions 'by themselves' in areas like care and management of sick animals, quantity of feed to be given to milch and other animals, selling of milk and milk products, size of the poultry, healthy management of poultry, type and quantity of feed to poultry and selling of eggs and birds.

Majority of medium farm women were seen to be involved in 'decision' making in consultation with their husbands/head of the families, in case of choice of crops/enterprises, use of family labour, storage of produce, number of animals to be maintained, sale and

Table 11 : Areas and decision making pattern of farm women

Sl. No.	Decision making area	LARGE FARM WOMEN (N = 25)					MEDIUM FARM WOMEN (N = 65)					SMALL FARM WOMEN (N = 90)				
		Wife	W+H	W+F	W+H+ F+N+ FR	HUS	Wife	W+H	W+F	W+H+ F+N+ FR	HUS	Wife	W+H	W+F	W+H+ F+N+ FR	HUS
1.	Choice of crops/	—	2	—	2	21	16	35	2	—	12	3	72	—	—	15
	enterprises	—	(8.0)	—	(8.0)	(84.0)	(24.6)	(53.8)	(3.1)	—	(18.5)	(3.3)	(80.0)	—	—	(16.7)
2.	Selection of seeds	—	2	—	2	21	18	14	2	—	31	24	39	6	6	15
		—	(8.0)	—	(8.0)	(84.0)	(27.7)	(21.5)	(3.1)	—	(47.7)	(26.6)	(43.3)	(6.7)	(6.7)	(16.7)
3.	Hiring of farm labour	2	12	—	—	11	16	18	—	—	31	16	74	—	—	—
	for different operations	(8.0)	(48.0)	—	—	(44.0)	(24.6)	(27.7)	—	—	(47.7)	(17.8)	(82.2)	—	—	—
4.	Decision on the use of	17	6	—	—	2	32	33	—	—	—	66	24	—	—	—
	family labour	(68.0)	(24.0)	—	—	(8.0)	(49.2)	(50.8)	—	—	—	(73.3)	(26.7)	—	—	—
5.	Storage of produce	—	6	2	—	17	20	37	2	—	6	48	42	—	—	—
		—	(24.0)	(8.0)	—	(68.0)	(30.8)	(56.9)	(3.1)	—	(9.2)	(53.3)	(46.7)	—	—	—
6.	Selling of surplus farm	—	2	2	—	21	—	14	—	—	51	—	75	—	—	15
	produce	—	(8.0)	(8.0)	—	(84.0)	—	(21.5)	—	—	(78.5)	—	(83.3)	—	—	(16.7)
7.	Quantity of grain/vegetables	—	2	2	—	21	—	18	—	—	47	—	75	—	—	15
	to be disposed of	—	(8.0)	(8.0)	—	(84.0)	—	(27.7)	—	—	(72.3)	—	(83.3)	—	—	(16.7)
8.	No. of animals to be	—	23	2	—	—	—	35	2	—	28	15	75	—	—	—
	maintained	—	(92.0)	(8.0)	—	—	—	(53.8)	(3.1)	—	(43.1)	(16.7)	(83.3)	—	—	—
9.	Sale and purchase of	—	6	2	—	17	—	14	2	49	—	45	—	—	—	45
	draught animals	—	(24.0)	(8.0)	—	(68.0)	—	(21.5)	(3.1)	(75.4)	—	(50.0)	—	—	—	(50.0)

(Contd.)

Table 11 . *(Contd.)*

Sl. No.	Decision making area	LARGE FARM WOMEN (N = 25)					MEDIUM FARM WOMEN (N = 65)					SMALL FARM WOMEN (N = 90)				
		Wife	W+H	W+F	W+H+ F+N+ FR	HUS	Wife	W+H	W+F	W+H+ F+N+ FR	HUS	Wife	W+H	W+F	W+H+ F+N+ FR	HUS
10.	Sale and purchase of	—	11	2	—	12	—	41	2	—	22	—	75	—	—	15
	milch animals	—	(44.0)	(8.0)	—	(48.0)	—	(63.1)	(3.1)	—	(33.8)	—	(83.3)	—	—	(36.7)
11.	Care and management of	9	10	2	—	4	55	2	—	8	—	81	9	—	—	—
	sick animals	(36.0)	(40.0)	(8.0)	—	(16.0)	(84.6)	(3.1)	—	(12.3)	—	(90.0)	(10.0)	—	—	—
12.	Quantity of feed to be	2	17	—	—	6	37	22	2	4	—	81	9	—	—	—
	given to milch and	(8.0)	(68.0)	—	—	(24.0)	(56.9)	(33.8)	(3.1)	(6.2)	—	(90.0)	(10.0)	—	—	—
	other animals															
13.	Decision on artificial	—	—	2	7	16	2	2	2	59	—	—	—	12	69	9
	insemination to animals	—	—	(8.0)	(28.0)	(64.0)	(3.1)	(3.1)	(3.1)	(90.7)	—	—	—	(13.3)	(76.7)	(10.0)
14.	Selling of milk and	25	—	—	—	—	65	—	—	—	—	90	—	—	—	—
	milk products	(100)	—	—	—	—	(100)	—	—	—	—	(100)	—	—	—	—
15.	Deciding on size of	11	12	2	—	—	57	2	6	—	—	90	—	—	—	—
	poultry	(44.0)	(48.0)	(8.0)	—	—	(87.7)	(3.1)	(9.2)	—	—	(100)	—	—	—	—
16.	Type of breed to be	—	12	2	5	6	25	4	15	21	—	90	—	—	—	—
	maintained	—	(48.0)	(8.0)	(20.0)	(24.0)	(38.5)	(6.2)	(23.0)	(32.3)	—	(100)	—	—	—	—
17.	Health and management	21	2	—	2	—	63	2	—	—	—	81	9	—	—	—
	of poultry	(84.0)	(8.0)	—	(8.0)	—	(96.9)	(3.1)	—	—	—	(90.0)	(10.0)	—	—	—

(Contd.)

Table 11 : *(Contd.)*

Sl. No.	Decision making area	LARGE FARM WOMEN (N = 25)					MEDIUM FARM WOMEN (N = 65)					SMALL FARM WOMEN (N = 90)				
		Wife	W+H	W+F	W+H+F+N+FR	HUS	Wife	W+H	W+F	W+H+F+N+FR	HUS	Wife	W+H	W+F	W+H+F+N+FR	HUS
18.	Type and quantity of feed to poultry	10	11	—	—	4	39	—	10	16	—	90	—	—	—	—
		(40.0)	(44.0)	—	—	(16.0)	(60.0)	—	(15.4)	(24.6)	—	(100)	—	—	—	—
19.	Selling eggs and birds	25	—	—	—	—	65	—	—	—	—	90	—	—	—	—
		(100)	—	—	—	—	(100)	—	—	—	—	(100)	—	—	—	—
20.	Decision on spending income from farm enterprises	—	21	2	—	2	—	65	—	—	—	—	66	9	—	15
		—	(84.0)	(8.0)	—	(8.0)	—	(100)	—	—	—	—	(73.3)	(10.0)	—	(16.7)

Notes: W = Wife alone, W+H = Wife and husband; W+F = Wife and family;
W+H+F+N+FR = Wife, husband, family, neighbours and friends; HUS = Husband alone

Note: Figures in parantheses indicate percentages

purchase of milch animals and spending income from farm enterprises.

The medium farm women took decision with regard to artificial insemination to animals after consulting husband, family, neighbours and friends.

However, the husbands/head of the families of medium farm women were the exclusive decision makers in respect of selling of surplus farm produce, quantity of grain/vegetables to be disposed and sale and purchase of draught animals.

Areas and decision making pattern of small farm women

A close insight into Table 11 shows the decision making pattern of small farm women involved in rice based farming system. A large majority (53-100%) of small farm women took decision 'by themselves' in areas like use of family labour, storage of produce, care and management of sick animals, quantity of feed to be given to milch and other animals, selling of milk and milk products, size of the poultry, type of breed to be maintained, health and management of poultry, type and quantity of feed to poultry and selling of eggs and birds.

Majority of small farm women were very much involved in 'taking decisions along with their husbands' in case of selection of crops/enterprises, hiring of farm labour, selling surplus farm produce, quantity of grain/vegetables to be disposed, number of animals to be maintained, sale and purchase of draught animals, sale and purchase of milch animals and spending income from farm enterprises.

The small farm women were also involved in taking decision on artificial insemination to animals along with their husbands, family, neighbours and friends.

In most of agricultural communities, women have an important role in decision making with regard to farm and farm related enterprises. Livestock raising and management related activities were predominantly rural women's responsibility. Major decisions regarding these activities were being taken by the women themselves. Women of all groups were also involved by their spouses in making decisions regarding agriculture and horticulture on issues like choice of crops/enterprises and spending of income gained from these enterprises.

Women play an important role in decision making in farm sector. The decision making role of farm women has been a subject of interest in the diffusion of agricultural innovations and acceptance of technological changes. Since women had the entire burden of managing the household, they motivate their husbands/family members to adopt modern technologies which will increase their farm income.

Women also tend to look at problems in their totality from the sowing of a crop to its ultimate utilization either as food, feed or raw material. Therefore, for an economically and ecologically sustainable agriculture, the involvement of farm women in the process of modernization of farming practices is absolutely essential. Moreover, the male members of the family in small holdings are looking out for remunerative source of employment putting agriculture in the second place, compelling farm women to shoulder the entire burden of managing the farm and related activities. In these circumstances, they are forced to take decisions on various aspects of farming by themselves in day-to-day activities.

In view of this the general impression that farm women do not actively participate in decision making in the areas identified cannot be agreed to and it can be safely concluded that farm women are slowly and steadily forging ahead in taking decisions even in crop related activities which were hitherto male domains.

Difference in decision making pattern among three groups of farm women in rice based farming system

F-test was employed to find out any significant difference in respect of decision making pattern among three groups of farm women in rice based farming system with the following hypothesis.

N.H. : There will be no significant difference in the scores of decision making pattern among three groups of farm women.

E.H. : There will be significant difference in the scores of decision making pattern among three groups of farm women.

Since the overall F-ratio value (10.0182) was greater than theTable 12, F-value at the corresponding degrees of freedom, the null hypothesis was rejected at 0.01 level of probability.

Table 12 : Difference in decision making pattern among three groups of farm women

Source of Variation	DF	Sum of squares	Mean squares	F-ratio
Groups	2	3066.6250	1533.3125	10.0182**
Error	177	27090.3125	153.0526	
Total	179	30156.9375		

** Significant at 0.01 level of probability.

Therefore, it may be summarised that there was significant difference among the scores of three groups of farm women in respect of decision making pattern.

The mean scores of three groups of farm women were arranged in descending order of magnitude with corresponding critical differences in order to know which pairs of groups differ significantly in decision making pattern.

	Small	Medium	Large
Means	76.53	70.14	65.44
C.D.	5.48	5.71	3.95

Thus, mean scores of decision making pattern between large and medium did not differ significantly which was indicated by a bar. Hence, it may be concluded that there was significant difference in the mean scores of large and small; and medium and small farm women groups in respect of decision making pattern in rice based farming system. In other words, the small farm women had the highest mean score, i.e., 76.53 and the large farm women had the least mean score of 65.44 in respect of decision making pattern (Fig.4).

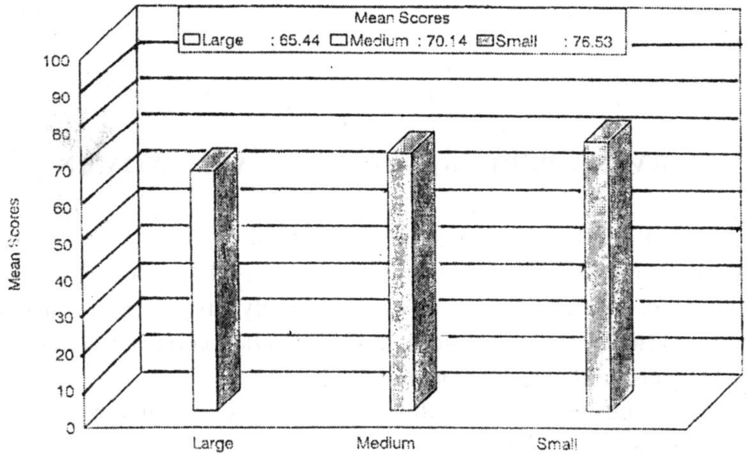

Fig 4 : Decision making pattern of farm women.

The findings were in the expected direction. In the patriarcheal society existing in the sampled area, the large and middle class women hardly come out of their homes leaving a very little scope to understand which enterprise is remunerative and which technologies are feasible and practicable for their situations and hence, unable to take decisions on their own. Moreover, the husband/ head of these families always expect these women just to carry out what they decide upon in all those areas where investment and expenditure are involved are jealously guarded and controlled by the men in the houschold despite the fact that women in these households are engaged in both productive and reproductive work. On the other hand, small farm women earn equally or sometimes more with/than their husbands and hence the small farm women take decisions on their own or sometimes consult their husbands. In this finding, the men and women of small farm families participated in the decision making process where situations are symmetrical, egalitarian or syncratic. This could be the plausible reason for the significant difference between small and large and medium farm women groups in decision making pattern in rice based farming system.

The finding differs with that of Shailaja (1990) who stated that there was no significant difference between large and small farm women in decision making.

SECTION – E

FARMING PERFORMANCE OF FARM WOMEN

The farming performance index developed by Rao (1985) was administered to the farm women in rice based farming system. The index constitute six components, namely, cropping intensity; crop yield index; milk yield index; level of adoption, commercialisation and expansion/diversification index.

The presentation of findings on this aspect is done under the following sub-heads:

Distribution of farm women on different components of farming performance.

Difference in cropping intensity among three groups of farm women.

Difference in crop yield index among three groups of farm women.

Difference in milk yield index among three groups of farm women.

Difference in level of adoption among three groups of farm women.

Difference in commercialisation among three groups of farm women.

Difference in expansion/diversification index among three groups of farm women.

Difference in overall farming performance among three groups of farm women.

Distribution of farm women on different components of farming performance

The data in Table 13 revealed the distribution of three groups of farm women on different components of farming performance.

Table 13 : Distribution of farm women on different components of farming performance

Sl. No.	Component and Category	Large (N=25) F	Large (N=25) %	Medium (N=65) F	Medium (N=65) %	Small (N=90) F	Small (N=90) %	Pooled sample (N=180) F	Pooled sample (N=180) %
1.	CROPPING INTENSITY :								
	Low	6	24.00	15	23.08	18	20.00	56	31.11
	Medium	18	72.00	35	53.84	54	60.00	95	52.78
	High	1	4.00	15	23.08	18	20.00	29	16.11
	Mean		112.68		110.30		100.26		105.61
	S.D.		8.19		17.16		14.74		15.86
2.	CROP YIELD INDEX :								
	Low	6	24.00	14	21.54	15	16.67	36	20.00
	Medium	15	64.00	40	61.54	54	60.00	120	66.67
	High	4	24.00	11	16.92	21	23.33	24	13.33
	Mean		109.64		107.16		92.10		99.97
	S.D.		21.57		16.18		16.26		18.72
3.	MILK YIELD INDEX :								
	Low	3	12.00	8	12.31	6	6.67	26	14.44
	Medium	16	64.00	49	75.38	75	83.33	136	75.56
	High	6	24.00	8	12.31	9	10.00	18	10.00
	Mean		79.52		98.09		97.51		95.22
	S.D.		17.14		11.68		12.04		14.15
4.	LEVEL OF ADOPTION :								
	Low	5	20.00	18	27.69	18	20.00	35	19.44
	Medium	14	56.00	33	50.77	60	66.67	117	65.00
	High	6	24.00	14	21.54	12	13.33	28	15.56
	Mean		60.84		60.63		48.30		54.49
	S.D.		12.45		11.27		9.00		12.05

(Contd.)

Table 13 : *(Contd.)*

Sl. No.	Component and Category	Groups of farm women							
		Large (N=25)		Medium (N=65)		Small (N=90)		Pooled sample (N=180)	
		F	%	F	%	F	%	F	%
5.	COMMERCIALISATION :								
	Low	3	12.00	14	21.54	18	20.00	39	21.67
	Medium	17	68.00	39	60.00	57	63.33	101	56.11
	High	5	20.00	12	18.46	15	16.67	40	22.22
	Mean		68.52		73.72		55.50		63.88
	S.D.		12.44		12.08		12.27		14.88
6.	EXPANSION/DIVERSIFICATION INDEX :								
	Low	3	12.00	22	33.84	24	26.67	42	23.33
	Medium	17	68.00	41	63.08	45	50.00	109	60.56
	High	5	20.00	2	3.08	21	23.33	29	16.40
	Mean		59.00		48.47		32.56		41.98
	S.D.		19.36		20.86		18.46		21.81

Cropping intensity: On perusal of Table 13, it is evident that majority of large farm women belonged to medium cropping intensity category followed by low (24.0%) and high (4.0%) cropping intensity categories.

With regard to medium farm women, 53.84 per cent of them fell into medium cropping intensity category followed by equal per cent of 23.08 per cent each of them in high and low categories.

In case of small farm women, 60 per cent of them belonged to medium cropping intensity category, while equal per cent of them (20% each) were in high and low categories.

Therefore, it can be concluded that majority of farm women in all the groups had medium cropping intensity.

Difference in cropping intensity among three groups of farm women

The data on each of the farming performance components and overall farming performance was analysed by applying F-test to find out the difference, if any, among the three groups of farm women. The results related to difference in cropping intensity among three groups of farm women is presented in Table 14.

N.H. : There will be no significant difference in the scores of cropping intensity among the three groups of farm women.

E.H. : There will be significant difference in the scores of cropping intensity among the three groups of farm women.

Table 14 : Difference in cropping intensity among three groups of farm women

Source of Variation	DF	Sum of squares	Mean squares	F-ratio
Groups	2	5221.6250	2610.8125	11.5643**
Error	177	39960.2500	225.7641	
Total	179	45181.8750		

** Significant at 0.01 level of probability.

Since the overall F-ratio value (11.5643) was greater than table value of 'F' with respect to the corresponding degree of freedom, the null hypothesis was rejected at 0.01 level of probability.

Hence, it can be concluded that there was significant difference among the scores of three groups of farm women in respect of cropping intensity.

Now, it is necessary to find out which group mean scores are differing significantly. For this purpose the means of three groups were arranged in descending order of magnitude as shown below. Then the difference between two mean scores were compared with the critical differences (C.D.).

	Large	Medium	Small
Means :	112.68	110.31	100.30
C.D. :	6.93	6.65	4.79

Thus, mean scores of cropping intensity between large and medium farm women did not differ significantly which was indicated by a bar. Therefore, it can be concluded that there was significant difference in mean scores of medium and small, large and small farm women with respect to cropping intensity. In other words, the small farm women had the lowest mean score, i.e., 100.30, while the large farm women had the highest mean score of 112.68 followed by medium farm women (110.31) in respect of cropping intensity.

Cropping intensity reflects the ability of a farm woman to utilise the land, labour, capital and technology efficiently to raise more number of crops per unit area per unit time to obtain higher productivity and income. The selected farm women in the study possessed family land with some source of irrigation facility to raise rice, a principal staple crop and other vegetable crops to augment the annual income. The land and other related sources being a worthy possession in rural areas, the farm women tried to put them into maximum utilisation to the best of their ability. This might be the reason that most farm women had medium cropping intensity. The finding had conformity with the findings of Rajini (1989) and Sreedevi (1996).

Significant difference was observed between the pairs of medium and small, large and small farm women with respect to cropping intensity. That means, the small farm women who are resource poor compared to medium and large could not raise more number of crops in an unit area in unit time. The present day agriculture has become very expensive with large amount of uncertainty because of vagaries of climate and market fluctuations in demand and supply which could have made the small farm women not to venture in aggressive agriculture and hence, the significant difference between small, medium and large farm women.

Crop yield index : It is clear from the data presented in Table 13 that most of the large farm women (64.0%) had medium crop yield index, while equal per cent of them (24.0%) had high and low crop yield index.

The data revealed that majority (61.54%) of medium farm women belonged to medium crop yield index category followed by 21.54 per cent low and 16.92 per cent in high crop yield index categories.

Among the small farm women, majority (60.0%) of them were in medium crop yield index category followed 23.33 per cent high and 16.67 per cent low crop yield index categories.

Hence, it may be summarised that most of the farm women in all groups had medium crop yield index.

Difference in crop yield index among the three groups of farm women

N.H. : There will be no significant difference in the scores of crop yield index among the three groups of farm women.

E.H. : There will be significant difference in the scores of crop yield index among the three groups of farm women.

Since the computed F-value (19.3093) was greater than the table value, the null hypothesis was rejected at 0.01 level of probability. Thus, it could be concluded that there was significant difference among the scores of three groups of farm women with respect to crop yield index (Table 15).

Table 15 : Difference in crop yield index among three groups of farm women

Source of Variation	DF	Sum of squares	Mean squares	F-ratio
Groups	2	11209.2500	5604.6250	19.3093**
Error	177	51375.2500	290.2557	
Total	179		62584.5000	

** Significant at 0.01 level of probability.

To confirm which group means differed significantly, the means of three groups were arranged in descending order of magnitude as shown below with the corresponding critical differences (C.D.) for comparison.

	Large	Medium	Small
Means :	109.64	107.9	92.1
C.D. :	7.85	7.54	5.43

It could be concluded that there was significant difference in mean scores of medium and small; large and small in case of crop yield index. In other words, the large farm women had the highest mean score, i.e., 109.64 while the small farm women had the lowest mean score of 92.1 in respect of crop yield index.

The selected farm women had raised other crops in their dry lands besides irrigated crops. The success of any crop in dry lands is uncertain as it depends on the vagaries of climate and hence, an element of risk is always considered by the farm women. In such circumstances, achieving the maximum overall crop yield index may not be possible for the farm woman of the region. Moreover, several studies indicated that majority of farm women were resource poor and could not afford to invest on modern technologies which are very expensive resulting in the non-exploitation of full potential of land, crop varieties, water and labour. Since, agriculture is the backbone of Indian economy where 70 per cent population had their living, the policy makers and administrators should give a serious thought to provide irrigation facilities, credit and other relevant inputs needed for crop production and see that farm women exploit the available resources to the maximum extent possible so as to put them into high crop yield index category. The finding has drawn support from the study of Sreedevi (1996).

There was significant difference between the mean scores of medium and small, large and small farm women in respect of crop yield index. The small farm women being illiterate had little chance to interact outside their social system. They are also not very much receptive to new innovations in agriculture and commercialised agriculture clubbed to expensive inputs might have made them not to invest in required amounts in the inputs like seed, fertilizer and pesticides resulting in low crop yield index when compared with large and medium farm women.

Milk yield index : Table 13 indicated that majority (64.0%) of the large farm women fell under medium milk yield index category followed by 24.0 per cent high and 12.0 per cent low milk yield index categories.

Regarding the medium farm women, most of them (75.38%) belonged to medium milk yield index category, while 12.31 per cent each were in high and low milk yield index categories.

In respect of small farm women, majority (83.33%) of them fell under medium milk yield index category followed by high (10.0%) and low (6.67%) milk yield index categories.

Thus, from the result it can be concluded that majority of farm women in all groups had medium milk yield index.

Difference in milk yield index among the three groups of farm women

N.H.: There will be no significant difference in the scores of milk yield index among the three groups of farm women.

E.H.: There will be significant difference in the scores of milk yield index among the three groups of farm women.

As the overall F-ratio value (29.5537) was greater than the table value, the null hypothesis was rejected at 0.01 level of probability.

Table 16 : Difference in milk yield index among three groups of farm women

Source of Variation	DF	Sum of squares	Mean squares	F-ratio
Groups	2	7223.8750	3761.9375	29.5537**
Error	177	22530.6250	127.2917	
Total	179	30054.5000		

** Significant at 0.01 level of probability

The mean scores of three groups of farm women were arranged in descending order with the corresponding critical differences in order to know which groups differ significantly.

	Small	Medium	Large
Means :	98.30	98.09	79.52
C.D :	3.59	4.99	5.20

The mean scores of milk yield index between medium and small did not differ significantly indicated by a bar. Hence, it can be concluded that there was significant difference in the mean scores of large and medium, large and small farm women in respect of milk yield index. It means that the small farm women had the highest mean score of 98.30 closely followed by medium farm women (98.09). The large farm women had the lowest mean score of 79.52 in respect of milk yield index.

It is also interesting to see that there was an increase in milk yield index as it goes from large to small. In other words, small followed by medium farm women concentrated more on this component than large farm women. It is clear that dairy is an excellent and profitable enterprise for all the groups of farm women which fits into the rice based farming system perfectly than any other in this region. The selected villages had milk collection centres posing least problems in disposal of milk. Several farm women began to concentrate on this enterprise which also helps them to augment their family income to improve their standard of living. The small and medium farm women had small holdings and crop husbandry alone may not provide sufficient income which will sustain throughout the year. Moreover, the lands which are not suitable for aerable cropping was used to raise green fodder for animals which helped them to bestow attention on this enterprise. Therefore, rural development agencies should strengthen the hands of farm women by providing more credit to maintain more milch animals (economic and feasible unit) and help to improve farming performance. This would certainly move farm women from the present medium to high milk yield index category.

Milk yield index is the milk yield of all milch animals in a homestead compared with average milk yields of the region. Significant difference was observed between the pairs of large and medium; large and small farm women in case of milk yield index. Though large farm women are involved in dairy activities, they differed significantly with others. These large farm women do not bestow personal attention in dairy activities leaving it to the mercy of labour or servants working on their farms, whereas medium and small farm women personally looked after these animals in providing green fodder, required quantity of fodder, concentrates and care and management of sick animals. Positive and effective results could be obtained in dairy when personal attention is bestowed upon as livestock enterprise is labour intensive. This could be the plausible reason for the significant difference between large, medium and small farm women in respect of milk yield index.

Level of adoption : The data in Table 13 revealed that majority (56.0%) of large farm women had medium level of adoption, while 24 per cent were in high and 20 per cent were in low adoption categories.

In case of medium farm women, most of them (50.77%) belonged to medium adoption level followed by low (27.69%) and high (21.54%) adoption categories.

With regard to small farm women, majority (66.67%) of them fell under medium adoption category followed by low (20.0%) and high (13.33%) adoption categories.

Hence, it can be concluded that majority of farm women in all groups had medium level of adoption.

Difference in level of adoption among the three groups of farm women

N.H. : There will be no significant difference in the scores on level of adoption among the three groups of farm women

E.H. : There will be significant difference in the scores on level of adoption among the three groups of farm women.

Table 17 : Difference in level of adoption among three groups of farm women

Source of Variation	DF	Sum of squares	Mean squares	F-ratio
Groups	2	6785.8125	3392.9062	31.5106**
Error	177	19058.5000	107.6751	
Total	179	25844.3125		

** Significant at 0.01 level of probability.

The over all F-ratio value (31.5106) was greater than the table value, the null hypothesis was rejected at 0.01 level of probability.

In order to know which groups differ significantly, the mean scores of three groups were arranged in descending order as shown below to compare with the corresponding critical differences (C.D.).

	Large	Medium	Small
Means :	60.84	60.47	48.30
C.D. :	4.78	4.59	3.31

The mean scores of level of adoption between large and medium do not differ significantly which was indicated by a bar. Therefore, it can be inferred that there was significant difference in the mean scores of large and small; medium and small farm women in respect of level of adoption. It means that the large farm women had the highest mean scores of 60.84, while the small farm women had the lowest mean score of 48.30 in respect of level of adoption.

Level of adoption was considered as the number of recommended practices followed for the principal crops grown on her farm and in dairy. The level of adoption of practices by the farm women depend on the feasibility of the technology. Since research and extension scientists tested the technologies for their feasibility before recommending to farmers resulting in adoption of most of the practices by farm women and hence, remained in the category of medium level of adoption.

Past several studies observed that the farm women had very little extension contact, extension participation and received no training either in agriculture or allied enterprises. How can women's efforts be made useful through developmental interventions positively to accelerate their growth? How can the policy makers and administrators be sensitised about gender issues in agriculture? Therefore, the exigency is that more women extension workers and officers should be employed in our extension system to increase women participation in agriculture resulting in high level of adoption. The main aim of research relating to agricultural technology, specially for women, should be labour diversification, drudgery reduction, improved energy conservation and higher and more stable income would certainly motivate the farm women of all groups from the present medium level of adoption to high level of adoption of technologies in agriculture and allied activities. The finding was similar to that of Umadevi (1992) and Sreedevi (1996).

Level of adoption was the number of recommended practices followed by a farm woman for the principal crops grown on her farm. The results revealed that the small farm women differed significantly with large and medium farm women in level of adoption. The small farm women were largely neglected by the extension agencies in transferring low cost or no cost technologies which otherwise could improve their level of adoption. It is quite obvious that extension agencies to reach their targets set forth by their higher ups in the administration always concentrated on the early adopters who undoubtedly are the large and medium groups of farm women. This has left the small farm women way behind giving no opportunity for them to become aware of new technologies. Moreover, the expensive technologies in the present day agriculture becoming inaccessible to these resource poor small farm women. Therefore, target group oriented research and extension is imperative to suggest simple and low cost technologies to the small farm women taking into consideration their limited available resources. This would certainly help to motivate the small farm women to adopt more recommended practices which subsequently help to improve their farming performance in rice based farming system.

Commercialisation : Table 13 indicated that most of the large farm women (68.0%) belonged to medium commercialisation category, while 20 per cent had high commercialisation. A small number (12.0%) of them had low commercialisation.

Among medium farm women, majority (60.0%) of them belonged to medium commercialisation category followed by low (21.54%) and high (18.46%) commercialisation categories.

With regard to small farm women, most of them (63.33%) fell under medium commercialisation category followed by low (20.0%) and high (16.67%) commercialisation categories.

Thus, from the results it could be concluded that majority of farm women in all groups had medium commercialisation.

Difference in Commercialisation index among the three groups of farm women

N.H. : There will be no significant difference in the scores of commercialisation index among the three groups of farm women.

E.H. : There will be significant difference in the scores of commercialisation index among the three groups of farm women.

In Table 18 the overall F-ratio value (43.9230) was greater than the table value, hence, the null hypothesis was rejected at 0.01 level of probability.

Table 18 : Difference in commercialisation index among three groups of farm women

Source of Variation	DF	Sum of squares	Mean squares	F-ratio
Groups	2	13136.3125	6568.1562	43.9230**
Error	177	26468.2500	149.5381	
Total	179	39604.5620		

** Significant at 0.01 level of probability.

The mean scores of three groups of farm women in descending order were given under along with their critical differences in order to know which groups are significantly differing.

	Medium	Large	Small
Means :	73.70	68.52	55.50
C.D. :	5.64	5.41	3.90

The mean scores between medium and large did not differ significantly indicated by a bar. Hence, it can be concluded that there was significant difference in the mean scores of medium and small; large and small farm women with respect to commercialisation index. In other words, the medium farm women had the highest mean score, i.e., 73.70 followed closely by the large farm women (68.52), while small farm women had the least mean score of 55.50 in respect of commercialisation index.

Commercialisation is a built-in mechanism of any farming system. The enterprises used by the farm women had high commercial value. The system adopted in this study was rice + vegetables + dairy. Rice being a staple food, the farm women had sold a little portion of total production. But she could sell major portion of vegetables and milk in the market on commercial lines to earn more income. Commercialisation is the percentage of produce sold from produce raised. More researches could be taken up to identify feasible farming systems by taking into consideration the available resources of the farmers and villages which have more commercial value in the market. Then, more number of farm women would certainly take to farming system approaches on scientific lines and develop high commercialisation attitude. The finding was in agreement with that of Sreedevi (1996).

A significant difference was observed between the small, medium and large farm women with respect to commercialisation index. This might be due to the fact that the small farm women who had limited crop and animal produce from their small holdings and with large family sizes may be just sufficient for their own consumption and leaving nothing or little to be marketed. With little or no monetary returns for their produce, it is quite natural that their commercialisation index was less than those of large and medium farm women.

Expansion/diversification index : It is evident from Table 13 that majority (68.0%) of large farm women had medium expansion/diversification index followed by high (20.0%) and low (12.0%) expansion index categories.

Regarding medium farm women, most of them (63.08%) belonged to medium expansion/diversification index category followed by low (33.84%) and high (3.08%) expansion/diversification index categories.

Among the small farm women, half (50.0%) of them belonged to medium expansion/diversification index category followed by low (26.67%) and high (23.33%) expansion/diversification index categories.

Thus, it can be summarised that majority of the farm women in all groups had medium expansion/diversification index.

Difference in expansion/diversification index among the three groups of farm women

N.H. : There will be no significant difference in the scores in expansion/diversification index among the three groups of farm women.

E.H. : There will be significant difference in the scores of expansion/diversification index among the three groups of farm women.

Table 19 : Difference in expansion/diversification index among three groups of farm women

Source of Variation	DF	Sum of squares	Mean squares	F-ratio
Groups	2	17960.6562	8980.3281	23.6506**
Error	177	67208.3120	379.7080	
Total	179	85168.9690		

** Significant at 0.01 level of probability.

In Table 19 the overall F-ratio value (23.6506) was greater than the table value, and hence, the null hypothesis was rejected by accepting the empirical hypothesis.

The mean scores of three groups of farm women were arranged in descending order to compare with critical differences (C.D.) to see the significant difference between the groups.

	Large	Medium	Small
Means :	59.00	48.47	32.56
C.D. :	8.98	8.63	6.21

The mean scores of all the groups differed significantly. Hence, it can be concluded that there was significant difference between the pairs, i.e., large and medium; medium and small; large and small with respect to expansion/diversification index. It means that the large farm women had the highest mean score of 59.0 followed by medium farm women (48.47). The small farm women had the lowest mean score, i.e., 32.56 in respect of expansion/diversification index.

Expansion is the degree of addition to the existing assets on the farm and off-farm enterprises. Farm women irrespective of group, i.e., large, medium and small take to diversified farming not only to take advantage of the complementary relationships between the enterprises but also as a device to reduce uncertainty. The farming system approach provides an opportunity or scope to the farm women to diversify and expand from the only activity agriculture to other related activities. This might be the fact that all farm women had medium expansion/diversified index. The small and scattered land holdings mainly under rainfed agriculture in conjunction with low per capita income had made agriculture a very poorly remunerative vocation. So, diversification in farm activities through farming systems approach certainly keep the farm women engaged or employed throughout the year and help them to increase their family income which subsequently raise their standards of living. Hence, the rural development agencies should make serious attempts to build necessary infrastructure in rural areas which would encourage farm women to move from the present medium to high expansion/diversification index. The finding did not agree with Sreedevi (1996) who observed that farm women had low expansion/ diversification.

The results reveal that there was significant difference between pairs, i.e., large and medium; medium and small; large and small in respect of expansion/diversification index. The large farm women with big farms, higher crop and animal production and other monetary resources can afford to expand/diversify their farm activities by spending large portion of income from the farm enterprises. Medium and small farm women with average and low farm income had to meet several expenses like household needs, farm needs and needs of social obligation, cannot invest much on expansion/diversification of their farm and non-farm enterprises. Hence, rural development agencies should help small and medium farm women to become accessible to credit sources on low or no interest rates to enable them to increase their expansion/diversification index.

Difference in the overall farming performance among the three groups of farm women

N.H. : There will be no significant difference in the scores of overall farming performance among the three groups of farm women.

E.H. : There will be significant difference in the scores of overall farming performance among the three groups of farm women.

In Table 20, the overall F-ratio value (16.5687) was greater than the table F-value. Hence, the null hypothesis was rejected at 0.01 level of probability.

Therefore, it can be concluded that there was significant difference among the scores of three groups of farm women in respect to overall farming performance.

Table 20 : Difference in overall farming performance among three groups of farm women

Source of Variation	DF	Sum of squares	Mean squares	F-ratio
Groups	2	199832.0000	99916.0000	16.5687**
Error	177	1067384.0000	6030.4180	
Total	179	1267216.0000		

** Significant at 0.01 level of probability.

In order to find out which group pairs are differing significantly, the mean scores of three groups were arranged in descending order of magnitude as shown below and compared with the critical differences (C.D.).

	Medium	Large	Small
Means :	495.10	492.80	427.84
C.D. :	35.81	34.41	24.77

The overall farming performance between medium and large did not differ significantly indicated by a bar. Hence, it was concluded that there was significant difference in the mean scores of medium and small; large and small farm women in respect of overall farming performance. In other words, the medium farm women had the highest mean score of 495.10 followed closely by large farm women (492.80). The small farm women had the least mean score of 427.84 in respect of overall farming performance (Fig. 5).

Farming performance

The overall farming performance is the farming productivity behaviour of farm women comprising six components, viz., cropping intensity, crop-yield-index, milk yield index, level of adoption, commercialisation index and expansion/diversification index in a rice based farming system. The results indicated that there was significant difference between small, medium and large farm women

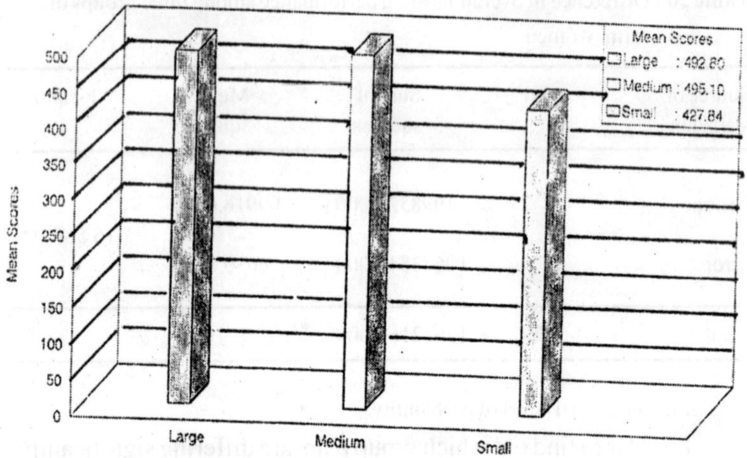

Fig. 5 : Difference in farming performance among three groups of farm women.

with respect to overall farming performance.In the earlier paragraphs, it was observed that small farm women had less cropping intensity, crop yield index, level of adoption, commercialisation and expansion/diversification index when compared to medium and large farm women. However, in case of milk yield index, small farm women were on par with medium but higher than the large farm women. This was the reason why the small farm women had low overall farming performance than medium and large farm women in rice based farming system.

The findings were contrary to the findings of Shailaja (1996) who reported that there was no significant difference between large and small farm women in mixed farming productivity.

SECTION – F

RELATIONSHIP BETWEEN SELECTED CHARACTERISTICS OF FARM WOMEN AND THEIR FARMING PERFORMANCE

This section deals with the nature of relationship observed between personal, socio-psychological and extension related characteristics of farm women and their farming performance in rice based farming system. This was determined with simple correlation analysis for the three groups of farm women and pooled sample. The findings are presented under the following heads :

1. Relationship between selected personal characteristics of farm women and their farming performance.
2. Relationship between selected socio-psychological characteristics of farm women and their farming performance.
3. Relationship between selected extension related characteristics of farm women and their farming.
4. Multiple regression analysis between selected independent variable and dependent variable farming performance.

To study these relationships, zero-order correlation coefficients between the scores on personal, socio-psychological and extension related characteristics of farm women and scores on their farming performance were computed. The findings are presented in the following pages.

Table 21: Simple correlation coefficient ('r' values) between selected characteristics of farm women and their farming performance

S.No.	Variable	Large (N = 25)	Medium (N = 65)	Small (N = 90)	Total (N = 180)
X_1	Age	0.3817NS	-0.2480*	0.2591*	0.0807NS
X_2	Education	0.0559NS	0.5725**	0.3395**	0.3907**
X_3	Farm size	0.3756NS	0.2006NS	0.4700**	0.3291**
X_4	Farming experience	0.3077NS	-0.1221NS	0.3488**	0.2458*
X_5	Material possession	-0.0295NS	0.2346NS	0.2480*	0.4050**
X_6	Annual income	0.7438**	0.8571**	0.4754**	0.5868**
X_7	Social participation	-0.0213NS	-0.0035NS	-0.0246NS	-0.0394NS
X_8	Innovativeness	0.7740**	0.9359**	0.5738**	0.7234**
X_9	Self-confidence	0.9288**	0.9189**	0.5866**	0.7822**
X_{10}	Level of aspiration	0.9120**	0.8747**	0.4621**	0.7470**
X_{11}	Scientific orientation	0.8465**	0.8316**	0.5178**	0.6497**

(Contd.)

Table 21 *(Contd.)*

X_{12}	Achievement motivation	0.9296**	0.8782**	0.5967**	0.7696**
X_{13}	Economic orientation	0.8767**	0.8625**	0.4239**	0.6969**
X_{14}	Risk preference	0.8923**	0.8563**	0.4758**	0.6938**
X_{15}	Rationality in decision making	0.9157**	0.8765**	0.5192**	0.7266**
X_{16}	Extension contact	0.7659**	0.7708**	0.6705**	0.7369**
X_{17}	Extension participation	0.5530**	0.4891**	0.1888NS	0.4962**
X_{18}	Training	0.6674**	0.6679**	0.4449**	0.5721**
X_{19}	Information seeking	0.8863**	0.7845**	0.4425**	0.6032**
X_{20}	Decision making pattern	0.8702**	0.8357**	0.5370**	0.5109**
X_{21}	Role performance	0.8752**	0.8271**	0.9359**	0.7286**

**Significant at 0.01 level of probability
*Significant at 0.05 level of probability
NS = Not significant

Relationship between personal characteristics of farm women and their farming performance

Age

N.H. : There will be no significant relationship between the scores on age and the scores on farming performance of farm women.

E.H. : There will be a positive and significant relationship between the scores on age and the scores on farming performance of farm women.

The computed correlation coefficient (r = 0.3817) was found to be non-significant in case of large women farmers and hence null hypothesis was accepted.

The 'r' value (-0.2480) was found to be negatively significant with medium farm women and had given a chance to accept the null hypothesis.

The correlation coefficient (r = 0.2591) was significant at 5 per cent level in case of small farm women. Hence, the null hypothesis was rejected and empirical proposition that there would be a positive relationship between the scores of age and the scores of farming performance of small farm women.

The computed (r = 0.0807) correlation coefficient for all groups of farm women together was not significant. Therefore, the null hypothesis stating that there will be no relationship between the age and the farming performance of farm women was accepted.

The non-significant relationship between age and farming performance is not surprising since many extension studies have shown that the age of the farmer/farm women does not really matter in farming performance. Similar observations were made by Sreedevi (1996).

Education

N.H. : There will be no significant relationship between the scores on education and the scores on farming performance of farm women.

E.H. : There will be a positive and significant relationship between the scores on education and the scores on farming performance of farm women.

The correlation 'r' values were found to be significant at 1 per cent level with respect to medium, small and farm women of all groups together. Hence, null hypothesis was rejected and can be concluded that there would be a significant and positive relationship between education and farming performance of farm women. The correlation coefficient (r = 0.0559) though not significant in respect of large farm women but in a positive direction.

Education was found to have non-significant relationship with farming performance in case of large farm women. Generally, the educated large farm women in rural areas do not come out of their houses and never participate in farming activities. They spend time by reading weekly and monthly journals and novels. This might be the reason for their non-significant relationship. The finding is in conformity with Rani (1988). Education had significant relationship with farming performance in respect of medium, small and pooled sample. Education opens up many avenues to the farm women to learn new things about farming resulting in better farming performance and it is true in case of medium and small farm women as they physically and mentally participate in almost all farming activities. The observations are in agreement with that of Shailaja (1990) and Sreedevi (1996).

Farm size

N.H. : There will be no significant relationship between the scores on farm size and the scores on farming performance of farm women.

E.H. : There will be a positive and significant relationship between the scores on farm size and the scores on farming performance of farm women.

The correlation coefficients were positively significant in respect of small and all-farm women groups together. Hence, null hypothesis was rejected and concluded that there would be a positive and significant relationship between farm size and farming performance. The 'r' values in case of large and medium farm women though not significant but are in a positive direction.

The farm size was found to have non-significant relationship with farming performance in respect of large and medium farm women. The increase in the farm size results in less concentration on farm activities because the farm would become unmanageable especially in the present context where serious farm labour shortage is widely felt. Similar observation was reported by Seema (1986). However, a positive and significant relationship was observed between farm size and farming performance in case of small and pooled sample of farm women. Large farm size leads to more produce and surpluses to support innovations and introduction of technological changes. This might be the plausible reason for their relationship. The findings were in agreement with that of Shailaja (1990).

N.H. : There will be no significant relationship between the scores on farming experience and the scores on farming performance of farm women.

E.H. : There will be a positive and significant relationship between the scores on farming experience and the scores on farming performance of farm women.

The computed correlation coefficients were not significant in case of large and medium farm women. Therefore, null hypothesis was accepted.

The correlation 'r' value (0.3488) in respect of small farm women was found to be significant at 1 per cent level and 'r' value (0.2458) of all farm women groups together was also significant at 5 per cent level. Hence, null hypothesis was rejected and empirical proposition that there would be a positive and significant relationship between the scores on farming experience and the scores on farming performance of farm women was accepted.

Farming experience was not significantly related with the farming performance of large and medium farm women. Farming experience do not matter for these farm women as their participation in farm and related activities were not encouraging. Even the experienced farm women do not come out of their houses to perform farm activities as they feel it below their dignity and prestige. Hence, this non-significant relationship. However, farming experience was significantly related with farming performance of small farm women and pooled sample. With more experience in farming, one naturally performs a better job on the farm. The small farm women who are resource poor cannot have high farming performance, but by gaining more experience she would be able to understand the complex nature of technologies, with great discrimination and selectivity and, choose only those enterprises or technologies that would reward her in augmenting the family income. The findings were in agreement with that of Goud (1990).

Material possession

N.H. : There will be no significant relationship between the scores on material possession and the scores on farming performance of farm women.

E.H. : There will be a positive and significant relationship between the scores on material possession and the scores on farming performance of farm women.

In case of large farm women the 'r' value showed negative and non-significant relationship while, correlation coefficient of medium farm women was also non-significant relationship and hence null hypothesis was accepted.

The computed 'r' values in respect of small farm women and all farm women groups together were positive and significant at 5 per cent and 1 per cent levels respectively. Therefore, null hypothesis was rejected by accepting empirical proposition that there would be a positive and significant relationship between the scores on material possession and the scores on farming performance of farm women.

There was a positive and significant relationship between material possession and farming performance in case of pooled sample of farm women. The more the material possession the more the socio-economic status. This higher status in the village society enables them to get new information more easily. The more the material possession like bullocks, implements, tractor, etc. enable the farm women to perform the most difficult and time consuming field operations very easily. This might help them to grow more crops in a year and adopt recommended practices resulting in more farming performance. The results were similar to the findings of Reddy (1996).

Annual income

N.H. : There will be no significant relationship between the scores on income and the scores on farming performance.

E.H. : There will be a positive and significant relationship between the scores on income and the scores on farming performance.

The correlation coefficients 'r' values of large, medium, small and all farm women groups together were found to be significant at 1 per cent level. Hence, null hypothesis was rejected by accepting the empirical proposition that there would be a positive and significant relationship between annual income and the farming performance of farm women in rice based farming system.

Annual income was found to have positive and significant relationship with farming performance of large, medium, small and pooled sample of farm women. The farm women of high annual income would not find it difficult to invest on purchasing of inputs like improved seeds, fertilizer, pesticides etc., to get increased yields. They would become more risk bearing in adopting new technologies and might join the elite group 'early adopters' and reap windfall profits.

The findings has drawn support from the study of Shailaja (1990).

Relationship between socio-psychological characteristics of farm women and their farming performance

Social participation

N.H. : There will be no significant relationship between the scores on social participation and the scores on farming performance of farm women.

E.H. : There will be a positive and significant relationship between the scores on social participation and the scores on farming performance of farm women.

The computed correlation coefficients 'r' values were negatively non-significant in respect of large, medium, small and all farm women groups together. Hence, the null hypothesis was accepted. The data did not support the original proposition that there would be a positive and significant relationship between the scores on social participation and the scores on farming performance of farm women.

In this study, very few farm women had social participation and this has not affected their farming performance in anyway. In the present day social context, more social participation, i.e., member/ president of village panchayat, cooperative society etc. will have deleterious effect on farming and related activities as the individuals always look for the benefits of such offices or positions and farming would become a secondary occupation. This might be the possible reason for its negatively non-significant relationship. The findings were nearer to the findings of Sreedevi (1996).

Innovativeness

N.H. : There will be no significant relationship between the scores on innovativeness and the scores on farming performance of farm women.

E.H. : There will be a positive and significant relationship between the scores on innovativeness and the scores on farming performance of farm women.

The correlation coefficient 'r' values were 0.7740, 0.9359, 0.5738 and 0.7234 in case of large, medium, small and all farm women groups together respectively. These values were found to be positively significant at 1 per cent level. Hence, null hypothesis was rejected accepting the empirical proposition and concluded that there would be a positive and significant relationship between the scores on innovativeness and the scores on farming performance of farm women.

Past studies and experiences indicated that an innovative farmer always reaped windfall profits from new technologies. An innovation in farming has the potential to exploit new markets and thereby the innovator/early adopter can command the markets and get high and most remunerative prices for her produce. This might be the plausible reason for the significant relationship between innovativeness and farming performance of farm women. The results were supported by the studies of Shailaja (1990).

Self-confidence

N.H. : There will be no significant relationship between the scores on self-confidence and the scores on farming performance of farm women.

E.H. : There will be a positive and significant relationship between the scores on self-confidence and the scores on farming performance of farm women.

The computed correlation coefficients for different groups were, large (0.9288): medium (0.9189), small (0.5866) and all farm women groups together (0.7822). These 'r' values were found to be positive and significant at 1 per cent level. Therefore, empirical proposition was accepted rejecting null hypothesis and concluded that there will be a positive and significant relationship between scores on self-confidence and the scores on farming performance of farm women.

Confidence in one's own-self would strengthen the determination of a farm woman to forge ahead of others in adopting new technologies, utilise all the available resources at her command resulting in increased farming performance. The self-confidence makes the farm women feel that they are second to none and do not care for negative criticism. This might be the reason for the significant relationship between self-confidence and farming performance. The finding has drawn support from the studies of Rao (1985).

Level of aspiration

N.H. : There will be no significant relationship between the scores on level of aspiration and the scores on farming performance of farm women.

E.H. : There will be a positive and significant relationship between the scores on level of aspiration and the scores on farming performance of farm women.

The computed correlation coefficients were found to be significantly related in case of large, medium, small and all farm women groups together. Hence, the null hypothesis was rejected accepting the empirical hypothesis concluding that there would be a positive and significant relationship between the scores on level of aspiration and the scores on farming performance of farm women.

A farm woman or anyone will aspire to reach great heights in the chosen profession, i.e., farming and related activities in this study. This becomes possible only when a farm woman converge all her efforts, i.e., physical, mental and monetary to put into farming and related activities. In other words, farm woman should put her heart and soul in her profession resulting in high farming performance and increased income. Similar studies were reported by Shailaja (1990).

Scientific orientation

N.H. : There will be no significant relationship between the scores on scientific orientation and the scores on farming performance of farm women.

E.H. : There will be a positive and significant relationship between the scores on scientific orientation and the scores on farming performance of farm women.

Table 21 reveals that the correlation coefficients ('r' values) in case of large, medium, small and all farm women together were found to be positively significant at 1 per cent level of probability. Therefore, the null hypothesis was rejected and empirical proposition that there would be a positive and significant relationship between the scores on scientific orientation and the scores on farming performance of farm women was accepted.

The plausible reason might be that an individual with high scientific orientation try to accept improved agricultural technologies and evaluate them more objectively and adopt those technologies which satisfy their needs in their farms with more accuracy than others. An individual with scientific orientation tend to look at the basket of choices on technologies, enterprises and farming systems given to her and choose the most appropriate, relevant and feasible ones to improve her farming performance and farm income. The finding was in agreement with that of Shailaja (1990).

Achievement motivation

N.H. : There will be no significant relationship between the scores on achievement motivation and the scores on farming performance of farm women.

E.H. : There will be a positive and significant relationship between the scores on achievement motivation and the scores on farming performance of farm women.

The 'r' values, 0.9296, 0.8782, 0.5967 and 0.7696 in respect of large, medium, small and all farm women together were found to be positively significant at 1 per cent level. Hence, the empirical proposition was accepted by rejecting the null hypothesis and concluded that there would be a positive and significant relationship between the scores on achievement motivation and the scores on farming performance of farm women.

These farm women try to compare themselves with the other farm women in their villages and try to exhibit their excellence in the field activity. This urge for development among farm women might have resulted in their frequent verbal interactions to gain more knowledge and experience. This might have made the farm women to perform better in rice based farming system. The finding was in line with that of Shailaja (1990).

Economic orientation

N.H. : There will be no significant relationship between the scores on economic orientation and the scores on farming performance of farm women.

E.H. : There will be a positive and significant relationship between the scores on economic orientation and the scores on farming performance of farm women.

Table 21 indicates that the 'r' values on economic orientation of large, medium, small and all farm women together had shown a positive and significant relationship with farming performance. Hence, null hypothesis was rejected concluding that there would be a positive and significant relationship between the scores on economic orientation and the scores on farming performance of farm women.

Economic orientation refers to the extent to which an individual is oriented towards getting high economic ends such as maximisation of farm profits. This orientation plays an important role in shaping the development of an individual. With the idea of getting maximum profit the farm women strive hard to maximise the production from their farm enterprises. It is obvious that farm women tend to undergo a process of change only when there happens to be a strong economic urge. At this juncture, the farm woman will commit herself to adopt all those feasible technologies which would give her higher economic returns. The finding was in concurrence with that of and Shailaja (1990).

Risk preference

N.H. : There will be no significant relationship between the scores on risk preference and the scores on farming performance of farm women.

E.H. : There will be a positive and significant relationship between the scores on risk preference and the scores on farming performance of farm women.

The computed correlation coefficients on risk preference clearly showed that 'r' values of large, medium, small and all farm women together had significant relationship with their farming performance. Thus, null hypothesis was rejected by accepting empirical hypothesis stating that there would be a positive and significant relationship between the scores on risk preference and the scores on farming performance of farm women.

The farm women of the study have adopted farming systems

approach by integrating crop and animal husbandry enterprises. Dependence only on crop husbandry is uncertain as it in turn is dependent on vagaries of climate. So, to avoid an element of risk the farm women have opted animal husbandry enterprise which certainly is not as uncertain as crop husbandry. The farm women are already in the right direction preferring to rise more than one crop and combination of enterprises on their farms to avoid any risk. This augurs well for the farm women to be motivated towards farming systems approach. The finding was contrary to the observations reported by Reddy (1990).

Rationality in decision making

N.H. : There will be no significant relationship between the scores on rationality in decision making and the scores on farming performance of farm women.

E.H. : There will be a positive and significant relationship between the scores on rationality in decision making and the scores on farming performance of farm women.

The data on rationality in decision making indicate that the 'r values of large, medium, small and all farm women together were found to be positively significant at 1 per cent level with farming performance giving a chance to reject null hypothesis by accepting empirical proposition and was concluded that there would be a positive and significant relationship between the scores on rationality in decision making and the scores on farming performance of farm women.

In this age of information explosion, several new agricultural and allied technologies are being diffused into agricultural communities. The farm woman is not in a position to pick up the right technologies at right time as the farm woman herself has not been exposed to cosmopolite sources of information. Therefore, there is every need to educate the farm women to develop scientific rationality while taking decisions. Cosmopolite sources like extension agencies should strive hard in this direction by employing more women extension workers. This also helps the farm women to get reinforcement to their knowledge regarding latest farm technologies.

The finding was concurring with that of Shailaja (1990).

Relationship between extension related characteristics of farm women and their farming performance

Extension contact

N.H.: There will be no significant relationship between the scores on extension contact and the scores on farming performance of farm women.

E.H. : There will be a positive and significant relationship between the scores on extension contact and the scores on farming performance of farm women.

The calculated 'r' values on extension contact 0.7659, 0.7708, 0.6705 and 0.7369 in respect of large, medium, small and all farm women together were found to be significant at 0.01 level of probability. Hence, null hypothesis was rejected by accepting empirical hypothesis stating that there would be a positive and significant relationship between the scores on extension contact and the scores on farming performance of farm women.

The possible reason might be that through extension contact with extension agencies, the farm women will be able to discuss the farm problems such as the incidence of pests, availability of improved seeds, availability of subsidised inputs etc. They will also be in a position to take proper action at the appropriate time which in turn increases the productivity of their farming enterprises. Similar findings were reported by Sreedevi (1996).

Extension participation

N.H. : There will be no significant relationship between the scores on extension participation and the scores on farming performance of farm women.

E.H. : There will be a positive and significant relationship between the scores of extension participation and the scores on farming performance of farm women.

The computed 'r' values of large, medium and all farm women together had significant relationship at 0.01 level of probability. Therefore, empirical hypothesis was accepted by rejecting null hypothesis. However, the data reveals that small farm women r value had no significant relationship but was in a positive direction. Hence, it could be concluded that there would be a positive and significant relationship between the scores on extension participation and the scores on farming performance of all farm women together.

By participating in extension activities such as exhibitions, farmers' days, kisan mela, demonstrations etc., the farm women will be able to come in contact with agricultural scientists, fertilizer dealers and other progressive farmers and gain first hand information by exchange of ideas with them. Since "seeing is believing", the new technologies exhibited while organising extension activities by the extension agency, the farm women will straightaway adopt those feasible technologies without any loss of time and increase their farm income. The finding was similar to that of Shailaja (1990).

Training

N.H. : There will be no significant relationship between the scores on training and the scores on farming performance of farm women.

E.H. : There will be a positive and significant relationship between the scores on training and the scores on farming performance of farm women.

The data in Table 21 shows that the correlation coefficients of large, medium, small and all farm women together were found to be positively and significantly related at 0.01 level of probability and hence, null hypothesis was rejected, while accepting the empirical proposition stating that there would be a positive and significant relationship between the scores on training and the scores on farming performance of farm women.

Training is one of the means by which desired changes in

knowledge and skills related to farming can be brought about. It is also possible that the farm women through training change their attitudes and motivate towards successful farming performance. Thus, the training has positive relationship with farming performance. The finding has drawn support from Sreedevi (1996).

Information seeking

N.H. : There will be no significant relationship between the scores on information seeking and the scores on farming performance of farm women.

E.H. : There will be a positive and significant relationship between the scores on information seeking and the scores on farming performance of farm women.

The computed correlation coefficients depicts that the 'r' values of large, medium, small and all farm women together had significantly related at 0.01 level of probability. Hence, null hypothesis was rejected as the data supports the original proposition that there would be a positive and significant relationship between the scores on information seeking and the scores on farming performance of farm women.

The farm women who are innovative and active try to seek information on improved seed varieties, practices, inputs and extension advice to enable them to perform better and maximise the profits on their farms. The result was in agreement with that of Sreedevi (1996).

Decision making pattern

N.H.: There will be no significant relationship between the scores on decision making pattern and the scores on farming performance of farm women.

E.H. : There will be a positive and significant relationship between the scores on decision making pattern and the scores on farming performance of farm women.

The calculated 'r' values in respect of large, medium, small and all farm women together were found to be positively significant at 0.01 level of probability with farming performance. Hence, empirical hypothesis was accepted by rejecting the null hypothesis and concluded that there would be a positive and significant relationship between the scores on decision making pattern and the scores on farming performance of farm women.

The decision-making of farm women has been a subject of some interest in the diffusion of agricultural innovations and acceptance of technological changes by them. In some cases of crop husbandry, it is the farm women who take decision regarding choice of crops and varieties to be used. Livestock rearing and management are predominantly farm women's responsibility. Most of the decisions regarding livestock raising are being taken by farm women themselves. The finding was in line with that of Shailaja (1990).

Role performance

N.H. : There will be no significant relationship between the scores on role performance and the scores on farming performance of farm women.

E.H. : There will be a positive and significant relationship between the scores on role performance and the scores on farming performance of farm women.

The computed 'r' values in the table 0.8752, 0.8271, 0.9359 and 0.7286 in respect of large, medium, small and all farm women together were found to be positively significant at 0.01 level of probability. Hence, null hypothesis was rejected by accepting the empirical proposition stating that there would be a positive and significant relationship between the scores on role performance and the scores on farming performance of farm women.

Farm women in these villages actively participated in majority of farm operations. Those farm activities in which women engaged include drying, storing and protection of farm produce, transplanting, weeding, thinning and gap filling, harvesting, threshing etc. Majority of animal related tasks were performed by women. Their active participation in agriculture, horticulture and animal husbandry has lad to increased farming performance and subsequently to improved productivity in their farms. The findings were concurring with the studies conducted by Shailaja (1990).

Multiple regression analysis between the selected independent variables and dependent variable—farming performance

In the previous section, each of the independent variables was hypothesized to have an amount of independent effect on the dependent variable, viz., farming performance of farm women. The relationship was expressed in terms of zero order correlation coefficient. However, farming performance was viewed, not as the effect of single independent factor but as the manifestation of combined influence of all the selected variables as part of an interdependent system, with their reciprocal and interactive relationships. Hence, in this section, a multiple regression analysis between selected independent variables and the dependent variable was carried out.

The following multiple regression equation was used in this investigation:

$$Y = a + b_1 x_1 + b_2 x_2 + b_3 x_3 + \ldots + b_k x_k$$

where,

a = constant

b_1 = partial regression coefficient which appears in the equation and represents the amount of change in Y that can be associated with a unit change in x_1, the remaining independent variables being held constant.

k = the number of independent variables.

The following symbols were used to denote the variables.

Y = Farming performance of farm women
X_1 = Age
X_2 = Education
X_3 = Farm size
X_4 = Farming experience
X_5 = Material possession
X_6 = Annual income
X_7 = Social participation
X_8 = Innovativeness
X_9 = Self-confidence
X_{10} = Level of aspiration
X_{11} = Scientific orientation
X_{12} = Achievement motivation
X_{13} = Economic orientation
X_{14} = Risk preference
X_{15} = Rationality in decision making
X_{16} = Extension contact
X_{17} = Extension participation
X_{18} = Training
X_{19} = Information seeking
X_{20} = Decision making pattern
X_{21} = Role performance

The multiple correlation coefficient represents the Zero order correlation between the actual farming performance (Y) and the predicted farming performance (K), from multiple regression equation. The predictive power of multiple regression equation was evaluated with the help of the square of the multiple correlation coefficient R^2 (the coefficient of determination). The coefficient of determination represents the proportion of the total variation explained by the variables taken together in the regression equation.

The prediction power of the multiple regression equation was tested by using 'F' test.

$$F_K\,(N\text{-}K\text{-}1) = \frac{R^2}{1\text{-}R} \times \frac{N\text{-}K\text{-}1}{K}$$

With K, (N-K-1) d.f.

where.

R^2 = Coefficient of determination
N = Number of farm women in the sample
K = Number of independent variables

After determining the significance of the multiple regression coefficient, the contribution of each independent variable was taken up.

The significance of each of the partial regression coefficients in multiple regression equation was determined by using the student's t-test:

$$t = \frac{b}{\text{SE of (b)}}$$

where,

b = Partial regression coefficient.

SE of (b) = Standard error of the partial regression coefficient.

Then, the independent variables which contributed most to the prediction of farming performance were determined by comparing the standard partial regression coefficients called 'beta weights' of the respective independent variables in the regression equation. It may be mentioned that in measurement of independent variables, different scales were used. Therefore, a comparison of a unit of change in one variable with a unit of change in another becomes meaningless if partial regression coefficients alone were used, inas much as they were a function of the respective scales. To enable comparision of the partial regression coefficients, a correction was made by standardizing each partial regression correction was made by standardizing each partial regression coefficient by utilizing the standard deviation of each variable.

A standardized (or adjusted) partial regression coefficient was called the 'beta weight' of that partial regression coefficient. The formula for deriving beta weight was :

$$\text{Beta weight} = \frac{\text{S.D. of independent variable}}{\text{S.D. of dependent variable}} \times \begin{array}{c}\text{Partial}\\ \text{regression}\\ \text{coefficient}\end{array}$$

In this study, all the twenty-one independent variables, i.e., X_1 to X_{21} were used in the multiple regression equation to predict the farming performance of large, medium, small and all farm women together.

Multiple regression analysis between selected independent variables and dependent variable — farming performance of large farm women

General Hypothesis

Farming performance of large farm women can, in part, be predicted from twenty-one independent variables.

In other words, the scores on the twenty-one independent variables will explain a significant amount of variation in the scores of farming performance.

The statistical hypothesis stated in the null form was 'the additional sum squares for regression added by the variable X_1 to X_{21} is zero'. In Table 22, R^2 was 0.7933 which indicated that 79.3 per cent variation in the farming performance was explained by all the twenty-one variables together.

The coefficient of determination (R^2) obtained above was significant at 0.05 level of probability ($F = 21.69$).

Table 22 : Multiple regression analysis between selected independent variables and Dependent variable — farming performance of large farm women

(N = 25)

S.No.	Independent variable	Beta weight of standardized partial regression coefficient	Regression coefficient	't' value of partial regression
X_1	Age	-2.8746	-2.9920	0.5710NS
X_2	Education	-0.4323	-0.4460	0.0153NS
X_3	Farm size	-2.909	-3.0313	1.3504**
X_4	Farming experience	0.3675	3.4487	1.0698**
X_5	Material possession	-8.3108	-8.3369	0.6608NS
X_6	Annual income	0.0638	0.7337	0.1086NS
X_7	Social participation	0.0379	4.1284	0.1420NS
X_8	Innovativeness	-14.1991	-14.2254	1.3150**
X_9	Self-confidence	1.6668	42.2060	1.1163**
X_{10}	Level of aspiration	-0.7360	-1.7539	0.0321NS
X_{11}	Scientific orientation	0.4682	51.7430	1.5675**
X_{12}	Achievement Motivation	-29.4339	-29.4947	1.4387**
X_{13}	Economic orientation	0.0754	12.3819	0.2550NS
X_{14}	Risk preference	0.4319	9.7854	0.7043NS
X_{15}	Rationality in decision making	1.1066	21.8164	0.7240NS
X_{16}	Extension contact	-32.9552	-32.9680	0.9161*
X_{17}	Extension participation	0.1309	14.0611	0.8082NS
X_{18}	Training	0.4593	32.9942	1.8556**
X_{19}	Information seeking	-25.6000	-25.6487	1.1555**
X_{20}	Decision making pattern	0.4412	2.8544	1.3973**
X_{21}	Role performance	0.3154	1.9119	0.6241NS

$R^2 = 0.7933$*

F_{21} = 3 d.f. calculated value = 21.69

Thus, the null hypothesis was rejected and it could be concluded that the combined contribution of twenty-one independent variables was significant in predicting the farming performance of large farm women.

Multiple regression analysis between selected independent variables and dependent variable — farming performance of medium farm women

General hypothesis

Farming performance of medium farm women can, in part, be predicted from twenty-one independent variables.

Stated in other words, the scores on the twenty-one independent variables will explain a significant amount of variation in the scores of farming performance of medium farm women

In Table 23, R^2 was 0.9472 which indicated that 94.7 per cent variation in the farming performance of medium farm women was explained by all the twenty-one variables together.

The coefficient of determination (R^2) obtained above was significant at 0.01 level of probability.

Thus, the null hypothesis was rejected and was concluded that the combined contribution of twenty-one independent variables was significant in predicting the farming performance of medium farm women.

Table 23 : Multiple regression analysis between selected independent variables and dependent variable — farming performance of medium farm women

(N = 65)

S.No.	Independent variable	Beta weight of standardised partial regression coefficient	Regression coefficient	't' value of partial regression
X_1	Age	0.7759	7.4330	4.0167**
X_2	Education	-6.8570	-6.8658	0.9452**
X_3	Farm size	0.0962	6.9472	1.4890**
X_4	Farming experience	-4.5374	-4.6139	12.0415**
X_5	Material possession	0.2112	8.9678	2.4112**
X_6	Annual income	0.3434	8.4680	1.7900**
X_7	Social participation	0.0259	5.6880	0.4222**
X_8	Innovativeness	0.5694	14.5191	2.2338**
X_9	Self-confidence	0.6477	14.1655	1.8007**

(Contd.)

Table 23 *(Contd.)*

X_{10} Level of aspiration	0.2548	16.8558	1.1478**
X_{11} Scientific orientation	-16.1885	-16.1996	0.9324**
X_{12} Achievement Motivation	-12.2782	-12.3360	1.2552**
X_{13} Economic orientation	-81.6270	-81.6367	2.6688**
X_{14} Risk preference	0.6499	19.2518	1.8675**
X_{15} Rationality in decision making	0.3060	6.8050	1.1239**
X_{16} Extension contact	0.2088	16.9350	1.7580**
X_{17} Extension participation	-8.4046	-8.4140	0.7920**
X_{18} Training	-8.6617	-8.6728	0.8922**
X_{19} Information seeking	0.2640	4.9323	1.2866**
X_{20} Decision making pattern	-2.1577	-2.3384	2.6508**
X_{21} Role performance	0.1687	1.0909	1.8784**

$R^2 = 0.9472$**

$F_{21} = 43$ d.f. calculated value = 36.74

Multiple regression analysis between selected independent variables and dependent variable — farming performance of small farm women

General Hypothesis

Farming performance of small farm women can, in part, be predicted from twenty-one independent variables.

In other words, the scores on the twenty-one independent variables will explain a significant amount of variation in the scores of farming performance of smallo from women.

In Table 24.R^2 was 0.9544 which indicated that 95.4 per cent variation in the farming performance of small farm women was explained by all the twenty-one variables together.

The coefficient of determination (R^2) obtained above was significant at 0.01 level of probability.

Thus, the null hypothesis was rejected and concluded that the combined contribution of twenty-one independent variables was significant in predicting the farming performance of small farm women.

Table 24 : Multiple regression analysis between selected independent variables and dependent variable – farming performance of small farm women

(N = 90)

S.No.	Independent variable	Beta weight of standardised partial regression coefficient	Regression coefficient	't' value of partial regression
X_1	Age	0.0491	0.6141	0.7243**
X_2	Education	0.0892	9.5676	0.7840**
X_3	Farm size	-15.1744	-15.1826	2.4800**
X_4	Farming experience	0.1465	1.9161	2.7586**
X_5	Material possession	0.1636	11.0156	1.7315**
X_6	Annual income	-1.6630	-1.7247	0.7774**
X_7	Social participation	-2.6808	-2.6870	0.3516**
X_8	Innovativeness	0.9574	14.3997	1.1436**
X_9	Self-confidence	0.1684	3.2133	0.1948NS
X_{10}	Level of aspiration	0.1013	14.6806	0.5280**
X_{11}	Scientific orientation	-12.5520	-12.5755	1.2957**
X_{12}	Achievement motivation	0.0481	0.6828	0.1320NS
X_{13}	Economic orientation	-39.7427	-39.7542	2.7506**
X_{14}	Risk preference	-8.9083	-8.9449	1.1053**
X_{15}	Rationality in decision making	-10.7425	-10.7898	1.4244**
X_{16}	Extension contact	-35.0924	-35.1029	1.8585**
X_{17}	Extension participation	0.0211	4.3150	0.4270**
X_{18}	Training	0.0892	8.3889	0.8765**
X_{19}	Information seeking	0.4888	6.2523	3.9605**
X_{20}	Decision making pattern	0.0158	0.1143	0.0550NS
X_{21}	Role performance	1.0131	5.2484	14.3741**

R^2 = 0.9544**

F_{21} = 68 d.f. calculated value – 67.76

Multiple regression analysis between selected independent variables and dependent variable — farming performance of pooled sample of farm women

General Hypothesis

Farming performance of all farm women together can, in part, be predicted from the twenty-one independent variables.

Stated in other words, the scores on the twenty one independent variables will explain a significant amount of variation in the scores of farming performance of pooled sample of farm women.

In Table 25, R^2 was 0.8799 which indicated that 87.9 per cent variation in farming performance of pooled sample of farm women was explained by all the twenty-one variables put together.

Table 25 : Multiple regression analysis between selected independent variables and dependent variable — farming performance of pooled sample of farm women

(N = 180)

S.No.	Independent variable	Beta weight of standardised partial regression coefficient	Regression coefficient	't' value of partial regression
X_1	Age	0.1384	1.5343	2.3969**
X_2	Education	0.1739	18.6905	3.8162**
X_3	Farm size	—1.0642	—1.1477	1.2156**
X_4	Farming experience	—0.8655	—0.9444	1.3204**
X_5	Material possession	0.1407	3.6751	1.7931**
X_6	Annual income	0.1009	1.0299	0.8985**
X_7	Social participation	—11.0171	—11.0230	1.9005**
X_8	Innovativeness	0.7924	11.6511	5.0156**
X_9	Self-confidence	0.1200	2.5528	0.5733**
X_{10}	Level of aspiration	0.2170	15.8299	3.2022**
X_{11}	Scientific orientation	—37.3767	—37.3939	7.1733**
X_{12}	Achievement Motivation	0.3574	5.8692	1.7895**
X_{13}	Economic orientation	—45.0028	—45.0144	4.8041**
X_{14}	Risk preference	—4.3243	—4.3586	1.2879**
X_{15}	Rationality in decision making	-1.1079	-1.1520	0.4488**
X_{16}	Extension contact	-0.0434	-0.0544	0.0092NS
X_{17}	Extension participation	0.0794	10.1351	1.8318**
X_{18}	Training	0.0670	6.3557	1.3242**
X_{19}	Information seeking	0.1199	1.9864	1.4413**
X_{20}	Decision making pattern	-0.0501	-0.2044	0.4319**
X_{21}	Role performance	0.5717	3.3812	11.5433**

$R^2 = 0.8799$**

F_{21} 158 d.f. calculated value = 55.13

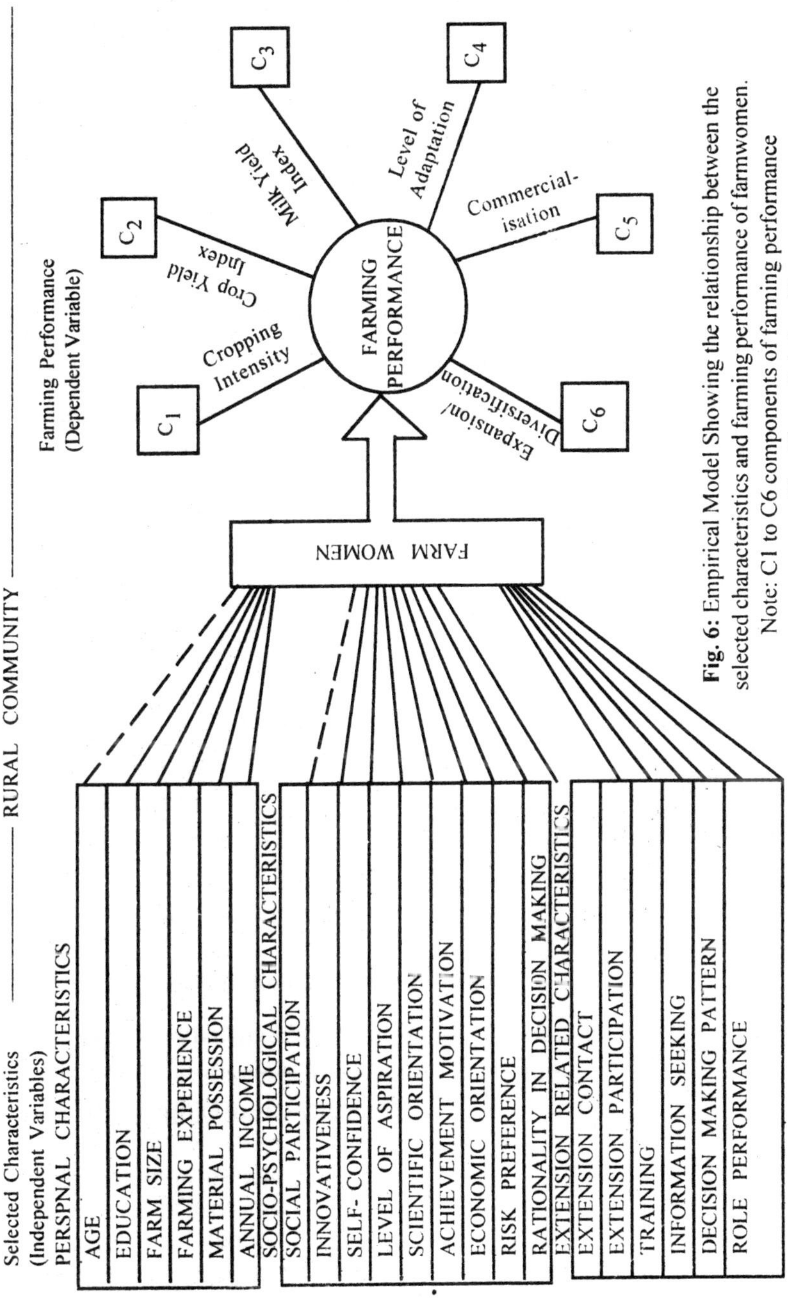

Fig. 6: Empirical Model Showing the relationship between the selected characteristics and farming performance of farmwomen.

Note: C1 to C6 components of farming performance

—— Significant Relationship

------ Non-Significant Relationship

The coefficient of determination (R^2) obtained above was significant at 0.01 levelof probability.

Thus, the null hypothesis was rejected and it could be concluded that the combined contribution of twenty-one independent variables was significant in predicting the farming p.rformance of pooled sample of farm women.

G. EMPIRICAL MODEL OF THE STUDY

A conceptual model was developed (Fig. 1) to analyse the variables related to the farming performance of farm women in rice based farming system. The relationship was tested by means of correlation coefficient analysis. On the basis of results of analysis, the empirical model was developed and presented in Fig. 6.

5

SUMMARY AND CONCLUSION

Any understanding of the process of production particularly agriculture and related production would remain incomplete if the roles and farming performance of women are not analysed. Women in the rural areas form the most important productive workforce in the national economics of majority of developing nations including India. In India, as high as 76 per cent of rural population is engaged in agricultural production and rural women comprise about 50 per cent of agricultural workforce. According to 1991 census, India has 20 per cent of women cultivators. Their participation in agriculture and related activities has been silently appreciated but women are hardly assisted or vocationally prepared for their active involvement in the development process. By and large, farm women remained as silent workers — 'invisible hands'.

A major reason for this is the failure of our developmental planning lies in treating women as 'end products' rather than 'agencies of change'. A substantial part of this mystification of the needs of women has occurred because many a times their role as producers of goods has been underestimated and they often been included under such generalised category as 'farmer's wives' and not as 'farm women'.

The present study was, therefore, undertaken with a view to demystify the productive role of women in rice based farming system — an integration of agriculture, horticulture and animal husbandry enterprises. The study was also considered necessary as the statistics revealed that women participation in agriculture in

Andhra Pradesh is 70-96 per cent (Singh, K.N., 1990). In this study an effort was made to analyse the role performance of farm women on family farms, their nature of decision making pattern in farming, role perception of farm women and their husbands and the overall farming performance of farm women in relation to certain characteristics under the given social framework. Hence, the present study entitled "An analysis of roles and farming performance of farm women in rice based farming system in Ranga Reddy district of Andhra Pradesh" was taken up with following objectives:

General objective

To study the roles and farming performance of farm women in a rice based farming system.

Specific objectives of the study

1. To find out the personal, socio-psychological and extension related characteristics of different groups of farm women in rice based farming system;
2. To ascertain the roles performed by different groups of farm women;
3. To study the role perception of farm women and their husbands;
4. To identify the areas and decision making pattern of different groups of farm women;
5. To measure the farming performance of different groups of farm women in rice based farming system; and
6. To ascertain the relationship between the farming performance and selected characteristics of farm women, if any, in rice based farming system.

With these objectives in view, the available literature was reviewed, analysed and synthesised to prepare a conceptual model for the study. An *ex post facto* design was used for conducting the present investigation in twelve villages of Ranga Reddy district of

Andhra Pradesh. A sample size of 180 farm women was selected from three groups based on their farm size by employing proportionate stratified random sampling method. Both independent and dependent variables were measured by using appropriate existing tools by making necessary modifications and also using the instruments developed by the researcher in the present investigation. The parametric statistical tests were used to analyse the data. The salient findings of the study are summarised below:

Personal, socio-psychological and extension related characteristics of different groups of farm women

1. Majority of large farm women were middle aged, can read and write only, with large farm size, having 18-28 years of experience in farming, high material possession, medium annual income and no social participation. Most of them belonged to medium category of innovativeness, self-confidence, level of aspiration, scientific orientation, achievement motivation, economic orientation but with high risk preference. Most of large farm women had medium rationality in decision making but low extension contact, extension participation and training. Majority of large farm women belonged to medium information seeking behaviour, medium decision making pattern and with medium role performance.
2. Majority of medium farm women belonged to middle age, illiterate, with 18-28 years of farming experience. They fell in the medium category in case of farm size, material possession, annual income, innovativeness, self-confidence, level of aspiration, scientific orientation, achievement motivation, economic orientation, risk preference, rationality in decision making, extension contact, information seeking behaviour, decision making pattern and role performance. Most of the medium farm women had no social participation with low extension participation and training.
3. Most of the small farm women were middle aged, illiterate, small farm size with 18-28 years of farming experience.

They belonged to medium category in respect of annual income, innovativeness, self-confidence, achievement motivation, risk preference, rationality in decision making, extension contact, information seeking behaviour, decision making pattern and role performance. However, majority of them had no social participation and most of them found to have low material possession, level of aspiration, scientific orientation, economic orientation, extension participation and training.

Roles performed by different groups of farm women

4. Roles performed most often by large farm women in rice based farming system with respect to agriculture were: drying the produce, storing the produce and protection of stored produce. In horticultural crops, they performed roles like selection of vegetable crops and watering the nursery. With respect to animal husbandry, mostly they performed roles such as milking, feeding animals, care and management of animals, marketing of milk and collection of eggs.
5. Medium farm women most often performed roles like seed treatment, seed soaking and spreading seed in the bed, weeding in nursery, pulling and carrying seedlings to the main field, transplanting, gap filling in the main field, weeding in the main field, harvesting, threshing, winnowing, drying, storing and protection of produce in agriculture. In horticulture, they performed roles such as nursery bed preparation, spreading seed in the bed, watering the nursery, pulling and carrying seedlings to the main field, transplanting, weeding, thinning, gap filling and harvesting. In case of animal husbandry, they attend to roles like milking, feeding animals, maintenance of cattle shed, care and management of animals, and marketing of milk.
6. Small farm women most often performed all the roles identified under agriculture, horticulture and animal husbandry enterprises.

7. There was significant difference among the three groups of farm women in respect of roles performed by them in rice based farming system. In other words, the medium farm women had the highest role performance in comparision to small and large farm women in rice based farming system.

Role perception of different groups of farm women and their husbands

8. The large farm women and their husbands perceived women roles in rice crop as most important in respect of post-harvesting roles such as drying, storing and protection of the produce. In horticulture, the most important roles according to them were: spreading seed in the bed, watering the nursery and preparation of vegetable products. With respect to animal husbandry, they perceived most important roles such as milking, feeding the animals, marketing of milk, preparation of milk products, feeding the poultry birds, maintenance of bird cages, collection of eggs, selection of eggs for hatching and caring of sick birds.

   There was no significant difference between farm women and their husbands in respect of role perception in the selected enterprises of rice based farming system.

9. The medium farm women and their husbands perceived women roles in rice crop as most important in case of seed soaking and spreading in the bed, weeding in the nursery, gap filling and post-harvest operations like threshing, winnowing, drying, storing and protection of produce. In respect of horticulture, the most important roles perceived by them were: spreading seed in the bed, watering the nursery, thinning and gap filling, harvesting and preparation of vegetable products. Majority of medium farm women and their husbands perceived as 'most important' the roles such as milking, feeding the animals, care and management of animals, marketing of milk, preparation of milk products, feeding poultry birds, maintenance of bird cages, collection

of eggs and caring of sick birds.

Further, it revealed that there was significant difference between medium farm women and their husbands in respect of role perception in agriculture. However, there was no significant difference between them in role perception with regard to horticulture and animal husbandry enterprises.

10. The small farm women and their husbands perceived all the women roles in rice crop as most important. Similar perception was expressed by them in respect of horticulture roles except preparation of vegetable products. The small farm women and their husbands also perceived that all the roles identified are most important in respect of animal husbandry enterprise.

    Further, it revealed that there was no significant difference between small farm women and their husbands in respect of role perception in the selected enterprises of rice based farming system.

Areas and decision making pattern of different groups of farm women in rice based farming system

11. The findings revealed that large farm women took decisions by themselves in areas like use of family labour, selling of milk and milk products, health and management of poultry and selling of eggs and birds. The large farm women were involved in taking decisions along with their husbands in areas such as number of milch animals to be maintained, quantity of feed to milch and other animals and spending of income from farm enterprises. However, the decisions like choice of crops/enterprises, selection of seeds, storage and selling of farm produce, sale and purchase of animals and artificial insemination to animals were the exclusive domains of the husbands of large farm women.
12. Medium farm women were self-decision makers in areas related to most of animal husbandry activities. They were also involved in taking decisions along with their husbands in respect of choice of crops/enterprises, use of family

labour, storage of farm produce, number of animals to be maintained, sale and purchase of milch animals and spending of income from farm, while decisions on selling of surplus farm produce, selling of vegetables and sale and purchase of milch animals and spending of income from farm, while decisions on selling of surplus farm produce, selling of vegetables and sale and purchase of draught animals were exclusively taken by their husbands.

13. Small farm women were sole decision makers in areas such as use of family labour, storage of produce, care and management of animals, quantity of feed to be given to milch and other animals, selling of milk and milk products, size of the poultry type of breed to be maintained, health and management of poultry and selling of eggs and birds. These women were also involved in making major decisions on selection of crops/enterprises, hiring of farm labour, selling surplus farm produce and vegetables, sale and purchase of milch and draught animals and spending of income from farm enterprises.
14. Further, the data revealed that there was significant difference among the three groups of farm women in respect of decision making pattern. In other words, the small farm women had the better decision making pattern in rice based farming system than large and medium farm women.

Farming performance of farm women

15. The findings revealed that there was significant difference in the mean scores among the three groups (large, medium and small) of farm women in respect of cropping intensity, crop yield index, milk yield index, level of adoption, commercialisation index and expansion/diversification index. Thus, it could be summarised that the large farm women had the highest mean scores in respect of cropping intensity, crop yield index, level of adoption and expansion/ diversification index, while the medium farm women had

the highest mean scores with regard to commercialisation and overall farming performance than the other two groups. However, the small farm women had the highest mean score in respect of milk yield index in comparision to medium and large farm women.

16. The data also revealed that there was significant difference in the mean scores among the three groups (large, medium and small) in respect of overall farming performance. In other words, the medium farm women had the better overall farming performance than the large and small farm women in rice based farming system.

Relationship between the selected characteristics of farm women and their farming performance

17. There was a positive and significant relationship between the characteristics of farm women, namely, education, farm size, farming experience, material possession, annual income, innovativeness, self-confidence, level of aspiration, scientific orientation, achievement motivation, economic orientation, risk preference, rationality in decision making, extension contact, extension participation, training, information seeking, decision making pattern and role performance with their farming performance.
18. The combined contribution of twenty-one independent variables (characteristics of farm women) was significant in predicting the farming performance of three groups (large, medium and small) of farm women.
19. The selected twenty-one independent variables were able to explain 87.9 per cent variation in the farming performance of pooled sample of farm women.

Implications of the study

The farm women as 'Principal Cultivators' toil day long and are just able to subsist their families through small farm incomes. There are, however, limitations to women's ingenuity when the socio-cultural environment prevails against them. Still farm women have demonstrated extraordinary resilience and creativity in responding to the given situations. Therefore, based on the research findings, the following implications were proposed for the improvement of farming performance of farm women in rice based farming system.

The results of the present study revealed that majority of farm women were illiterate with small land holdings, low material possession with low to moderate annual incomes. Three-fourths of farm women had no social participation and majority were with low aspiration, extension contact, extension participation, information seeking and most of them had not received training. These shortcomings are the outcomes of the patriarchal values and asymmetrical situations enforced by tradition and rural society.

1. *The society* should be transformed through awareness on gender issues. As a component of strategy for development of women, a comprehensive sensitisation programme need, to be introduced through mass media, campaigns etc. to generate awareness about their own abilities among the farm women and to concretise their contribution to agriculture and related activities.
2. *Education* is a powerful tool in social transformation. It increases the understanding of the changing situations and broadens mental outlook and facilitate to interact within and outside their social system. Education makes them more receptive to new innovations in agriculture and allied fields which would in turn enhances their farming performance. Hence, sincere efforts must be taken by the governmental and non-governmental agencies to step up the functional and adult literacy programmes to the farm women as well as to their husbands.
3. *Training of farm women* – farm women require a variety of new knowledge and skills so that they could become self-confident and self-reliant. This could possibly be achieved through appropriately designed "Target Group Training (TGT)' programmes. The following aspects need

special consideration in Target Group Training (TGT):

- Identification of the actual training needs (knowledge; skill) of individuals or group of farm women.
- Designing appropriate training programmes. These may be short time and practice based programmes.
- Selecting the right type of participants (heterogeneous or homogeneous groups).
- Choice of the training institutes – may be government or non-government organisations.
- Training should be conducted as far as possible in the same village to which farm women belong.
- The training content should also include supervision, management and entrepreneurial development skills apart from crop and animal husbandry skills.
- Senior women officers should be positioned at the state and district levels to properly coordinate women's training needs.

4. Special extension services are a must to improve the farming performance of farm women. Extension services should:

- Upgrade the skills of existing extension workers in the improved technologies required by farm women.
- At least 25 per cent of the farm women should be selected as contact farmers in each VEO circle, if necessary by reconstituting the existing groups.
- Help organise farm women groups where community action is required.
- Frequent visits should be made to the villages by the extension officers to keep up the farm women's motivation.
- An integrated extension approach may be followed to enhance the farming performance of farm women. This includes:
  — identification of those systems or combinations

of rice enterprises that are profitable, compatible and acceptable to the farm women of a given location besides ensuring a desirable eco-balance.

— increasing the competency of the extension workers at all levels in terms of not only crop production technologies but also several other components of rice related enterprises and human relation skills.
— resorting to appropriate extension methods with more emphasis on 'Target Group Approach' instead of contact farmer approach.
— educating and motivating the farm women to resort to integrated land use methods and to increase the utilisation of local or internal resources. Such an attempt will lay a strong foundation for sustainable rice based farming system.

5. *Extension participation* – 'Seeing is believing' new approaches are to be followed in transfer of technology. These approaches enable the farm women to participate in large numbers and see the technologies for themselves which also help to formalise symbolic adoption. The approaches could be:

- *Farm women fairs:* Farm women will have a chance to see and interact with the scientists and extension officers to gain first hand information on new, relevant and feasible technologies. Efforts should be made to attract large number of farm women to these fairs.
- *Farm women clubs:* Non-governmental and governmental agencies should establish women clubs and encourage large membership in these farm women clubs. This forms the best forum for the women to meet, exchange ideas and problems. The meetings of the club should be attended by experts of different disciplines to solve the problems of peasant women in rice based farming system.
- *Farm women publications:* can be planned and brought

out by the concerned development departments for the benefit of farm women on different rice based farming systems.

- *PRA approach*: Need to work with farm women on Participatory Rural Appraisal (PRA) approach. This will enable the extension officers to have an insight into their working conditions and enable them to empathise and provide necessary development interventions for the empowerment of farm women.

6. *Information seeking* : Past studies and the present research indicated that farm women had not received any information directly from the institutional sources or formal sources. They depend only on informal sources for obtaining necessary information was found most credible and trustworthy. Hence, due thought should be given to appoint women extension officers as communicators or change agents. This step will undoubtedly accelerate the learning process among the farm women. The highly skilled female communicators will certainly have an additive effect on change in knowledge and skills of the farm women relating to agriculture, horticulture and animal husbandry technologies.
7. Since the 'feminisation process' in role performance in agriculture and allied activities is gaining emphasis from the study, the importance and need of human resources through training and acquisition of skills in the selected enterprises in rice farming system is inevitable and essential. Therefore, the planners, researchers and administrators have to see that the relevant knowledge and skills accessible to farm women to perform the identified roles with ease and efficacy which in turn would help them improve their performance in farming productivity.
8. The study has shown that the role perception of different groups of farm women was similar to their husbands in

the selected enterprises. Hence, the extension agencies should exploit the perseverance virtue of farm women and make efforts to strengthen them in all those areas where the perceptions of farm women and their husbands are similar to enhance the farming performance of farm women in the selected enterprises in rice based farming system.

9. The study revealed that though most of the decisions in animal husbandry and some decisions relating to agriculture and horticulture were taken by farm women, the most crucial and economic decisions like selling the produce and purchase of animals and inputs were exclusively decide by men only. Therefore, the planners should look at development in relation to equity for women if women have to be empowered in taking crucial decisions. The most important factor contributes towards this social change is the level of information disseminated among the rural farm women. The access to information would help them to achieve parity in the decision-making process. The feeling that if they are made equal shareholders in their husband's estate they will not only become effective decision makers in the family but will be able to contribute to rural development in a significant way.
10. Expansion or diversification of land based activities brings to focus the women's productive activities; so efforts should be made to help increase the farm income of women especially small and medium farm women to invest either in expansion or diversification of land based activities to improve farm productivity.
11. The relationships established in the study between the selected characteristics of farm women and their farming performance would serve as a guideline to the extension planners for manipulating the characteristics to derive improved performance in agriculture and other enterprises in rice based farming system.

Thus, various components for the development of farm women should be consistently monitored at each stage of progress which will certainly help the farm women to enhance their farming performance in rice based farming system.

Conclusion

The importance and need for the mobilization of human resources in rural development has been well recognised in almost the developing countries of the world today. An awareness of this need has also brought into prominence the role of women in increasing food production and the improvement of conditions of rural life. Women in agricultural societies are not only engaged in house-keeping and socialisation of the young but are also actively participating in the productive process. The foregoing analysis in this study amply supports this view and highlights the dominant role women play in agricultural and related production. The increasing participation of women in family farms leads to a process of 'feminisation of agriculture' and making the farm women as 'principal cultivators'.

The socio-cultural practices hinder women's mobility into non-agricultural occupations and tie them down to subsistence agriculture. As a result, although women perform most of the agricultural work and they are the best judges of new investments and bring changes necessary to modernize their agriculture and allied activities; yet invariably it is the men rather than the women who as head and owner of the family farm are the decision makers in vital matters. Therefore, a conscious effort should be made by the policy makers and the administrators in formulating strategies to involve women to improve their farming performance related to land based activities to enable them to move from subsistence agriculture to major income source for improved standards.

APPENDIX – I

RANK ORDER OF CHARACTERISTICS OF FARM WOMEN AND THEIR AVERAGE SCORES AS JUDGED BY EXPERTS

Rank	Characteristics	Average Score
A.	**Personal characteristics**	
1.	Experience in farming	2.70
2.	Annual Income	2.55
3.	Education	2.45
4.	Material possession	2.40
5.	Farm size	2.35
6.	Age	2.25
7.	Family type	2.02
8.	Family size	1.98
9.	Family norms	1.83
10.	Caste	1.40

$$\text{Weighted mean} = \frac{\text{Total score obtained for all items}}{\text{No. of items} \times \text{No. of respondents}} = 2.23$$

Rank	Characteristics	Average Score
B.	**Socio-psychological characteristics**	
1.	Achievement motivation	2.65
2.	Scientific orientation	2.63
3.	Innovativeness	2.60
4.	Risk preference	2.60
5.	Economic orientation	2.58
6.	Level of aspiration	2.55
7.	Self-confidence	2.43
8.	Social participation	2.43

Rank	Characteristics	Average Score
9.	Rationality in decision making	2.43
10.	Values related to agriculture	2.35
11.	Result orientedness	2.35
12.	Independence	2.18
13.	Cosmopolite orientation	2.15
14.	Conservatism–liberalism	1.93
	Weighted mean = 2.42	
C.	**Extension related characteristics**	
1.	Role performance of farm women	2.80
2.	Decision making pattern	2.78
3.	Training	2.70
4.	Extension contact	2.70
5.	Extension participation	2.60
6.	Information seeking	2.60
7.	Ability to coordinate farm activities	2.55
8.	Management orientation	2.48
9.	Mass media participation	2.43
10.	Knowledge of development programmes	2.43
	Weighted mean = 2.59	

Final list of characteristics of farm women selected for the study

1. Age
2. Education
3. Farm size
4. Farming experience
5. Material possession
6. Annual income
7. Social participation
8. Innovativeness
9. Self-confidence
10. Level of aspiration
11. Scientific orientation
12. Achievement motivation
13. Economic orientation
14. Risk preference
15. Rationality in decision making
16. Extension contact
17. Extension participation
18. Training
19. Information seeking
20. Role performance
21. Decision making pattern

BIBLIOGRAPHY

Bhuyan, B. and Tripathy, S.K., 1988. Role of women in agriculture – A study in Ganjam district of Orissa. *Journal of Rural Development*, July (4) : 445-452, NIRD, Hyderabad.

Devi, L. and Reddy, V., 1984. Role expectation and role performance of rural women in farm activities. *Indian J. Ext. Educ.* 20 (3 & 4) : 27-34.

Ghosh, *et al.*, 1988. Role of village women in decision making in different farm economic business. Bidhan Chandra Krishi Viswa Vidhyalaya, Mohanpur, Nadia, West Bengal.

Goud, M.P., 1990. *A study to measure entrepreneurial behavioural characteristics among small, medium and big farmers as related to their productivity.* M.Sc. (Ag.) thesis, APAU, Hyderabad.

Jhansirani, G., 1981. *Decision making patterns among rural families and type of participation by rural women in selected areas of decisions.* M.Sc. thesis, APAU, Hyderabad.

Lakshmi Devi, A., 1982. Role of rural women in agricultural development. *Kurukshetra*, Vol.XXX, No.2, Oct.16-31, p.17.

Lakshmi Devi, M.A., 1983. *Role expectation and role performance of rural women in farm and home management.* Ph.D. thesis, APAU, Hyderabad.

Mandal, *et al.*, 1989. Farming systems research in India – Strategies for implementation, NAARM, Hyderabad pp.16-17.

Mehta, P., Sharma, R.K. and Singh, J.N., 1980. Impact of mixed farming on economic efficiency of different farm sizes. *Indian J. Agric. Econ.* 30 (4): 166.

Mulay, S., 1988. Transfer of farm technology and its impact on farm women. International Conference on Appropriate Agricultural Technologies for Farm Women : Future Research Strategy and Linkage with Development Systems – Abstracts. Indian Coun. Agric. Res., New Delhi.

Padma, M., 1987. *An assessment of the nature and type of participation of women in rice cultivation practices in Agriculture with special reference to T & V system in A.P.* M.Sc. (Ag.) thesis, EEI, A.P. Agricultural University, Hyderabad.

Pudjiwati, S., 1987. Development in the role of Indonesian women in rural areas now changing from an agricultural to an industrial policy. Seminar on National Fungse Social Economic Walita, Indonesia, IPB, Bogor, 30 p.

Puneetha, P.S., 1989. *Role of women in rice cultivation.* M.Sc. (Ag.) Thesis, A.P. Agricultural University, Hyderabad.

Rajini, C., 1989. *A study on the extent of participation of degree of drudgery of farm women in crop production in Mahabubnagar district of A.P.* M.Sc. (Ag.) thesis submitted to APAU, Hyderabad.

Raj Mohini Sethi, 1991. *Women in Agriculture.* Rawat Publication, New Delhi, pp.1-5.

Raman, K.V., and Balaguru, T., 1990. Farming systems research in India – Strategies for implementation, NAARM,Hyderabad-18.

Rao, V.G.K., 1985. *A prediction analysis of farming performance of farmers through their entrepreneurial behavioural factors.* Ph.D. thesis submitted to APAU, Hyderabad.

Reddy, G.M., 1990. *A study on the participation of farm women in farm operations and decision making in vegetable production in Ranga Reddy district of A.P.* M.Sc. (Ag.) thesis, APAU, Hyderabad.

Reddy, V.R.K., 1996. *A critical analysis of dairy production technologies among the dairy farmers of East Godavari district of A.P.* Ph.D. thesis submitted to APAU, Hyderabad.

Sabitakumari, 1995. *Developmental priorities of rural women of*

Chandapur village in Medak district of A.P. M.Sc. (H.Sc.) thesis submitted to APAU, Hyderabad.

Samantha, R.K., 1994. They reap less than they sow. *The Hindu,* April 17, 1994.

Seema, B., 1986. *Role of farm women in the decision making process of a farming community in Trivandrum district.* Unpublished Thesis in Agrl. Ext. Kerala Agrl. University, Trivandrum.

Shailaja, S., 1990. *Role of women in mixed farming.* Ph.D. thesis submitted to UAS, Bangalore.

Singh, M.P., Sharma and Neeraj, 1988. Participation of women in different farm and household operations in the hills and western plains of U.P. Paper presented in a seminar organised by ICAR, IARI, New Delhi, Nov.30-Dec.4, 1988.

Singh, K.N. and Bhattacharya, H.C., 1990. *Crop production technologies for farm women – Women in Agriculture-technological perspective*, pp.59-60 & 94.

Sreedevi, R., 1996. *Gender analysis in managerial abilities and farming performance in K.G. Zone of A.P.* Ph.D. thesis submitted to APAU, Hyderabad.

Suchitra, D., 1987. *Role of women in commercial farming.* M.Sc. thesis, EEI, APAU, Hyderabad.

Surgeon, J.K., 1989. *A study on the management attributes of farmers as related to training performance in Ranga Reddy district of A.P.* M.Sc. (Ag.) thesis submitted to APAU, Hyderabad.

Swaminathan, M.S., 1990. *Farming systems research in India – Strategies for implementation,* NAARM, Hyderabad, pp.11-12.

Umadevi, B.K., 1992. *An analysis of impact of training and extension on farm women in WYTEP in Karnataka.* M.Sc. (Ag.) thesis submitted to APAU, Hyderabad.

Yadav, *et al.,* 1987. Women's empowerment – Global efforts and Indian initiatives. *Kurukshetra,* August, 1995.

_____ 1995. Women's empowerment – Global efforts and Indian initiatives. *Kurukshetra,* August, 1995.

INDEX